"*Revolutionizing Business Operation* at how to have best-in-class business operations. Tony and Filippo capture essential knowledge and critical insights in an actionable way that makes this a must-read book. I've seen firsthand the long-lasting value created by adopting these practices."

JOSUÉ ALENCAR, CEO, PersonoSprings Global, Brazil

"As every CEO and CIO knows, it is no longer sufficient for companies to just create winning products and services; they also ne d winning operations. This exciting book shows just how to achieve that."

RAUF ATES, founder of CEO Council, *Fast Company*, Turkey

"Knowing Saldanha and Passerini as industry thought leaders, I expected a profound book. I'm delighted that my expectations were wildly exceeded. As a Global Business Services leader, I have found practical and personal insights in this book. You need to hurry and get a copy of this book."

MATTIJS BACKX, Senior Vice President and Head of Global Business Services, PepsiCo

"For as long as I have known Tony and Filippo, they have pushed the boundaries of business transformation for competitive advantage. This book is a wonderful summary of their recipe."

AMIT BANATI, Chief Financial Officer, Kellogg Company

"Revolutionizing Business Operations is a fabulous guide. The three drivers the authors identify provide a practical and comprehensive approach to rethinking your business processes. Tony and Filippo have gained the respect of the business process industry first as executives, and now as the advisers."

VIVEK CHOUDHURY, Dean and Professor of Information Systems, Daniels College of Business, University of Denver

"Bravo to the authors! They have managed to mix highly sophisticated insights on lasting transformation with very compelling and practical stories. The ideas and resources in this book will leave a lasting legacy in the business operations industry."

SUZAN VAN DIJK, Senior Vice President, Global Business Services, Pandora

"The challenge for us in leading business and digital transformation is how to embed the right business drivers into our processes and systems. With this book Tony and Filippo do a fantastic job of giving us the secret sauce for dynamic business process transformation. *Revolutionizing Business Operations* is a must for anyone who wants to be successful in business or digital transformation."

HANS FRÖLICH, Senior Vice President, Global Business Services, EDGE Group

"Traditional operating model companies need a different mindset to accelerate value creation from their digital transformations. Tony and Filippo have distilled their knowledge from working with the largest companies in this simple and insightful new book. A must-read for executives."

CHAKRI GOTTEMUKKALA, cofounder and CEO, o9 Solutions

"An exceptional, practical, thought-provoking guide for creating dynamic, competitively superior corporate business processes across functions, business units, and geographies. Written by two brilliant pioneering veterans of P&G's groundbreaking Global Business Services unit, this book helps companies proactively transform in ways that are smarter, faster, and more innovative."

MICHELLE GREENWALD, Senior Partner, Descartes & Mauss, *Forbes* writer, and global conference and TEDx speaker

"This book is the next generation of the 1990s classic *Reengineering the Corporation*. Filippo and Tony do a fabulous job of getting us all to think about delivering operations through an enlightened 'go to market' or 'B to C' lens complete with prescriptive stages that allow each reader to develop and envision their very own custom pathway to a new dynamic and responsive operating model."

STEVE HOSLEY, Senior Vice President, Global Business Services, Estée Lauder Companies

"Business operations used to be thought of as back-room and boring, but now they are front-room, vital, and exciting. Rigid supply chains have transformed into flexible open market supply webs. This book shows you how to win in this new world."

BOB JOHANSEN, Distinguished Fellow, Institute for the Future, and coauthor of *Office Shock* and twelve other books

"It is hard to drive process transformation in an organization. It's even harder to stay in a state of constant transformation. And yet, that's what the current times require. This book shows you how to do both."

DR. FRANZISKUS KATH, Vice President, Emerging Technologies & Solutions, Johnson & Johnson

"An absolute must-read for anyone looking to improve their organization's efficiency and effectiveness, turning back-office processes into a competitive advantage."

ANASTASIA KOUVELA, Managing Director and Partner, Boston Consulting Group

"Filippo and Tony's unparalleled expertise and experience shine in the examples and clear approaches. This book is a huge milestone and a useful, thought-provoking read. Bravo!"

STEVE MCCRYSTAL, Chief Enterprise and Technology Officer, Unilever

"Whether you lead a private or public sector enterprise, one thing is a given. You must constantly transform your operating model or fall behind. Saldanha and Passerini share their proven secrets on how exactly this can be done. This isn't a theoretical model; it's a proven, practical approach to sustained competitive advantage."

KUMAR V. PRATAP, Senior Economic Adviser, Government of India

"*Revolutionizing Business Operations* is the ultimate cookbook for perpetual business transformation. What makes it even more delightful is that it's written in an engaging, easy-to-read manner. Filippo and Tony are the key thought leaders in the Global Business Services and business transformation space. This book is an opportunity to learn from the masters."

NAOMI SECOR, Global Managing Director, Shared Services & Outsourcing Network

"A strong business operation is the competitive edge that every company seeks in today's world. In this book Tony and Filippo distill the foremost strategies into easy actions. Best of all, their suggestions come from decades of actual leadership experience. This book is a must-read for planning a transformation journey."

YOICHIRO TAKAMI, Partner, EY Strategy and Consulting Co.

REVOLUTIONIZING
BUSINESS OPERATIONS

Best Wishes

Filippo

Amy S.

REVOLUTIONIZING
BUSINESS OPERATIONS

How to Build Dynamic Processes for
Enduring Competitive Advantage

Tony Saldanha and **Filippo Passerini**

Foreword by
Roger Martin

BK

Berrett–Koehler Publishers, Inc.

Berrett-Koehler Publishers, Inc.
1333 Broadway, Suite 1000
Oakland, CA 94612-1921
Tel: (510) 817-2277
Fax: (510) 817-2278
www.bkconnection.com

ORDERING INFORMATION

QUANTITY SALES. Special discounts are available on quantity purchases by corporations, associations, and others. For details, contact the "Special Sales Department" at the Berrett-Koehler address above.

INDIVIDUAL SALES. Berrett-Koehler publications are available through most bookstores. They can also be ordered directly from Berrett-Koehler: Tel: (800) 929-2929; Fax: (802) 864-7626; www.bkconnection.com.

ORDERS FOR COLLEGE TEXTBOOK / COURSE ADOPTION USE. Please contact Berrett-Koehler: Tel: (800) 929-2929; Fax: (802) 864-7626.

Distributed to the U.S. trade and internationally by Penguin Random House Publisher Services.

Berrett-Koehler and the BK logo are registered trademarks of Berrett-Koehler Publishers, Inc.

Printed in the United States of America

Berrett-Koehler books are printed on long-lasting acid-free paper. When it is available, we choose paper that has been manufactured by environmentally responsible processes. These may include using trees grown in sustainable forests, incorporating recycled paper, minimizing chlorine in bleaching, or recycling the energy produced at the paper mill.

Library of Congress Cataloging-in-Publication Data
Names: Saldanha, Tony, author. | Passerini, Filippo, author.
Title: Revolutionizing business operations : how to build dynamic processes for enduring competitive advantage / Tony Saldanha, Filippo Passerini ; foreword by Roger Martin.
Description: First edition. | Oakland, CA : Berrett-Koehler Publishers, [2023] | Includes bibliographical references and index.
Identifiers: LCCN 2023006152 (print) | LCCN 2023006153 (ebook) | ISBN 9781523003983 (paperback ; alk. paper) | ISBN 9781523003990 (pdf) | ISBN 9781523004003 (epub) | ISBN 9781523004010 (audio)
Subjects: LCSH: Organizational change. | Organizational effectiveness. | Strategic planning.
Classification: LCC HD58.8 .S2458 2023 (print) | LCC HD58.8 (ebook) | DDC 658.4/06—dc23/eng/20230216
LC record available at https://lccn.loc.gov/2023006152
LC ebook record available at https://lccn.loc.gov/2023006153

FIRST EDITION

30 29 28 27 26 25 24 23 | 10 9 8 7 6 5 4 3 2 1

Book production: BookMatters
Cover design: David Ter-Avanesyan

To our wives, Julia Saldanha and Lucia Passerini.
You make us better.

CONTENTS

FOREWORD

I met Filippo in November 2002 in unusual circumstances. A. G. Lafley, CEO of P&G at the time, had asked me to come to Cincinnati for a set of three meetings. He had done so at relatively the last minute, so he graciously sent the corporate jet to pick me up. He was facing a highly contentious decision about whether to do a major outsourcing of most services—IT, facilities management, HR, and procurement.

One group passionately believed that P&G should outsource the entire set of activities—desktop support, applications development, facilities management, payroll, and so on—to a major outsourcing firm. Another group felt equally strongly that it would be a terrible mistake to outsource any of these activities—P&G should manage them internally in a world-class fashion. Never an either/or guy, A.G. had asked Filippo to come back from an assignment running P&G marketing in Greece and develop a new, innovative alternative.

A.G. wanted each group to present their findings to me; I would then write him a memo with my recommendation. I had never had an assignment of that sort before and haven't had one like it since.

Filippo's approach called for the activities to be outsourced in three separate packages to best-of-breed outsourcing companies. His was the most compelling. That outsourcing, led by Filippo and his team, including Tony, would turn out to be the largest and among the most successful in the industry. Tony was program manager of the effort at the time. He had the job of managing the portfolio of the outsourcing projects and running the daily management of the program. Once the outsourcing deals were done, he would go on to design the governance of the outsourced work. When A.G. appointed Filippo as the new head of P&G Global Business Services (GBS), Filippo reached out to me to help him think through the GBS strategy going forward, through the outsourcing and beyond. I worked with Filippo and his team more intensively for the first few years of his time heading GBS and somewhat less so later. However, I always got to enjoy fabulous Italian dinners at Casa Passerini!

I think that *Revolutionizing Business Operations* is a terrific guide to process transformation. It is based on decades of practical experience in the trenches. But—and excuse my nerdiness—what I like best about it is that the model it puts forward embodies the characteristics of the outcome the authors desire. This is often not the case in business books. I will use my own field—strategy—to illustrate. Most would agree that strategy is a creative exercise aimed at making choices in a dynamic and uncertain environment. Strategy people often send me their models for creating strategy because they would like me to endorse or adopt them. The models tend to involve painfully laborious and bureaucratic processes—typically accompanied by complicated flow charts. While the desired output is a creative strategy, the model put forward is usually antithetical to creativity. In fact, the models are guaranteed to stomp out any hint of creativity when deployed.

In stark and wonderful contrast, *Revolutionizing Business Operations* is a book about dynamic transformation, and the book's core model does more than merely produce dynamic transformation—the model itself *embodies* dynamic transformation. I love that reinforcing consistency: a model for dynamism that itself is dynamic!

The authors' own journey illustrates the dynamism. When GBS was first applying this model (see Chapter 1), the most sophisticated and advanced thinking was what the authors now characterize as Stage 2 of the book's four-stage *Dynamic Process Transformation* model. But as of the writing of this book, the model has four stages, with the third and fourth having taken shape only as Filippo, Tony, and their colleagues utilized the then-existing model.

I would argue that the discovery of the two additional stages was a product of the dynamics of the model itself. Application of the model's core concepts drives learning and the discovery of more sophisticated models. For example, application of *Open Market Rules* for effectiveness in Stage 2 drives learning about new business capabilities, which helps move an organization from Stage 2—Effectiveness to Stage 3—Innovation. Application of the *Dynamic Operating Engine* drives learning on how to create a dynamic organizational DNA that helps move an organization from Stage 3—Innovation to Stage 4—Leadership (see Chapter 14).

I have little doubt that if the authors write an update of the book in ten years, there will be one or two more stages to the model they present. That is because as they use the book's model, its use will help them to learn and to advance their thinking. I have enjoyed watching the thinking thus far take shape and be laid out in this book, and I will be watching with great interest the further advances that its use will generate.

ROGER MARTIN, author, CEO adviser,
and #1-ranked management thinker

PREFACE

It is fascinating to see patterns emerge out of earlier, seemingly unrelated situations. That is how this book came about. After working for three decades or more each at Procter & Gamble, the two of us stayed in close touch in our next adventures. As we advised boards and Fortune 500 CXOs, or taught digital and process transformation, we kept swapping observations. Ruminating over the occasional beer in New York or Cincinnati, we started to notice similarities in the advice we were offering our respective clients. At first, we wondered whether this was due to experience bias (i.e., to a hammer, every problem looks like a nail). However, it became obvious quickly that this wasn't the case. There were indeed patterns in the problems faced in process operations and transformation. It was just that we could recognize them quickly, having lived through them as we developed and ran one of the biggest success stories in Global Business Services and IT transformation.

Then a second pattern emerged. The need to transform business processes was growing exponentially. This made sense, for it reflected a shift in the attitude of leaders regarding the importance of digitized and streamlined operations. Whether these operations are related to closing books, managing people, or operating supply chains, there is today a widespread urgency to transform them. Digitally native companies, especially those that play in the physical world, like Amazon, have demonstrated clearly that internal operational effectiveness can be a competitive advantage. The question for the two of us was what to do with that observation.

That's when we were struck by what was perhaps the most important set of patterns. All our advisory, teaching, and speaking work presented common patterns that would fit a finite set of models. Those patterns related to improving business processes in ways that we had developed intuitively and used at P&G and elsewhere. Those common patterns were the basis for what we kept advising others on. The demand for them told us they were relevant and helpful to others. We just needed to get those patterns out of our heads and into the open world.

That led to the formation of our company, Inixia. Through that company, we document, train, and certify executives from the largest organizations in the world on managing business operations and shared services. We apply the best, proven methodologies to professionalize operations. And while Inixia has been extremely successful, in time we felt that our work was incomplete. The approaches and models for revolutionizing business operations needed to be put further out into the open domain. In today's disruptive world, ideas and insights are resources that become more valuable if they can circulate freely and if others can build upon them. That's where this book comes in. It is our humble attempt to share our insights and resources so that others can benefit from, evolve, and improve the model for revolutionizing business operations. This is an important topic amid the fourth industrial revolution. We hope this book will add to the growing knowledge of how to thrive in this changing era.

This book is aimed at business leaders, public sector officials, and nonprofit managers. For simplicity in communications, it is addressed primarily to companies, but the concepts it contains also apply to public sector and nonprofit groups. The size of your organization and your level within it is immaterial. If your business has operations (whether they are related to finance, HR, or customer management), then you will find this book useful. There are clear patterns to how business operations can go beyond simple improvement and be transformed to become your secret weapon for winning consistently.

And best of all, you don't need to spend three decades to see the patterns.

To improve is to change;
to be perfect is to change often.

WINSTON CHURCHILL

Why *Dynamic Process Transformation?*

> **KEY INSIGHT**: Episodic process transformations are insufficient. Aim for continuous process transformation.

All organizations constantly sense and respond to changing needs; some are simply better at it than others. The oil company Shell did not start off in the energy industry; its origins in 1833 lay in trading seashells.[1] Nintendo, the electronic gaming company, began in 1889 as a playing card company, but, like Shell, it evolved over the decades. Companies evolve to consistently win in the marketplace in two ways—by creating winning products in line with shifting customer needs, and by improving their operations to get their products to customers more effectively. The focus of this book is on the latter. There is a way to create enduring competitive advantage by revolutionizing business operations. And it involves solving the challenge of creating unbeatable, constantly evolving business processes.

Some of you may challenge that assertion right away. Isn't a winning product much more important? After all, even if the Microsoft Zune MP3 player (remember that?) had been supported with the most effective business operation in the world, it would never have come close to the success of the legendary iPod. That is fair, and we'd like to be clear up-front that this isn't a case of either/or. Winning organizations evolve both products and business operations. Unfortunately, innovating on products tends to be sexier than transforming business operations. The former gets a disproportionate share of attention. We need to correct that—it is time to give transformational business operations their due.

Business Operations Grow Complex, Rigid, and Siloed with Time

The issue with the business processes of every company—in operations of product development, production, manufacturing, sales, finance, information technology, human resources, and so on—is that they quickly become obsolete due to ongoing changes in the marketplace, technology, or capabilities. These business processes grow more complex, rigid, and siloed over time. That sets up a dangerous sequence of events, as follows.

1. Business processes become obsolete.
2. One-off transformation programs are kick-started to reengineer, standardize, or automate processes. However, these rely on having the right prime mover to sense and sponsor this change.
3. Business transformation programs, even if initiated, fail to deliver 70% of the time.
4. Meanwhile, if an economic crisis, industry disruption, or global crisis occurs (e.g., the COVID-19 pandemic), the company is caught flat-footed by competitors who have already evolved their operations.

Sound familiar? It should, because this occurs in all types of organizations—big multinationals, small and medium-sized enterprises, government agencies, and nonprofits. This is inevitable, since it reflects the long-established business rule that "Organizations Are Organisms." And if organizations are indeed organisms, then these words should apply to business: "According to Darwin's *Origin of Species,* it is not the most intellectual of the species that survives; but the one that is able best to adapt and adjust to the changing environment in which it finds itself."[2] Our task, therefore, as leaders is to prepare for "survival of the fittest," not just by being episodically fit via periodic transformation programs, but by being continuously fit via *Dynamic Process Transformation*.

Introducing...*Dynamic Process Transformation*

So, if dynamic business processes are required, then how do you achieve them? To foster lasting evolution in internal operations, you need a mechanism to prevent business processes from becoming obsolete in the first place. You need a dynamic, living model for constant process evolution and optimization. The *Dynamic Process Transformation* model achieves that.

It addresses the issue because it gets to the root causes of the recurring obsolescence of business processes. First, even the best business process design can become stale if it doesn't constantly compare itself with the most disruptive new ideas across companies, and more importantly across industries. Second, functional business processes tend to be optimized within their silos. That is a problem, for it leads to suboptimization at the holistic end-to-end level. And finally, unless there is a disciplined methodology to drive this constant reoptimization to every person in the operation, it leads to episodic business transformation. These three root causes of obsolescence are important to note, because we will shortly base our three drivers of *dynamic processes* on them.

The *Dynamic Process Transformation* model provides self-improving, living transformation, which sets up a positive spiral of agility, efficiency, and effectiveness. Existing approaches of "transform –> get obsolete –> transform again" simply cannot deliver this. This becomes glaringly obvious during disruptive times, such as the 2019 pandemic. For most businesses, the COVID-19 pandemic highlighted their ability (or lack thereof) to change rapidly in the face of adversity. This was true of large behemoths like Amazon as well as local mom-and-pop retailers.

A local small business in Cincinnati, Ohio, had opened a wine shop just two months before the pandemic struck. With financial disaster looming, it relaunched itself as a successful wine and spirits home delivery business within a month. Whether it was a neighborhood shop or Amazon or Zoom videoconferencing, some businesses were clearly better positioned to turn adversity into opportunity. A major common thread across all these was the readiness of their internal operations to meet new customer realities.

Drivers That Make Business Processes Dynamic

Adaptable companies have specific qualities that result in dynamic business processes. Based on research into the differences between market leaders and laggards during economic crises, and our collective seven decades of experience in running Fortune 20 operations, we have crystallized them into three distinctive drivers of dynamic business processes (Figure 1). These are:

1. *Open Market Rules*

2. *Unified Accountability*

3. *Dynamic Operating Engine*

Open Market Rules for business processes: To understand the concept of *Open Market Rules*, let's contrast how most businesses work with their *external* customers, as opposed to how their functions, like finance and IT, work with their *internal* employees. Let's start with the fact that a business cannot compel its customers to buy products. Instead, it focuses on creating product value so that customers *want* its products. In contrast, internal functions rely heavily on mandating that their employees use particular business processes (e.g., they dictate the steps that must be followed to process a customer's order, and the software tool that must be used). To be clear, we are not about to suggest that the proven strategy of streamlining and standardizing business processes needs to be abandoned in favor of allowing every employee to do their

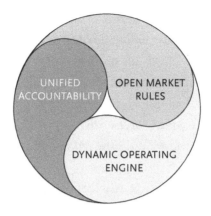

FIGURE 1: Drivers of *Dynamic Process Transformation*

own thing. Far from it. In fact, the word "rules" in the heading "*Open Market Rules*" was deliberately chosen to highlight the need for clear regulations. The point being made is that these rules need to be determined by open market competitive forces; overreliance on mandates and "one-size-fits-all" business processes must be avoided.

To be fair, when organizations first start to standardize their internal business processes, they may need to enforce certain specifications. For example, the templates used to process customer orders must have certain standard fields—order number, date, and so on. However, in our experience, this reliance on mandates and one-size-fits-all processes turns into a liability when some parts of the process need to change. When processes rely too heavily on mandates, the efficiency gained from top-down standards comes at the cost of ignoring valid change signals from employees, technology alternatives, and best-in-class benchmarks. This results in outdated business processes getting calcified, or in an unhealthy compromise between standardization and specific business needs.

Leaders of dynamic process operations use well-established and accepted *Open Market Rules* instead. They incorporate elements of the mindset that companies use *externally* with the consumers of their products. For instance, a consumer-centric company like Apple builds trust with its customers by being in touch with their needs, by constantly evolving product offerings, by being transparent about its products, and by effectively *pulling* the customers into their offerings. Apple couldn't possibly *push* the product onto them, nor would they want to. Similarly, dynamic process leaders will be mindful to blend the minimally mandated "push" of legal, ethical, and corporate standards with the open market forces arising from employees, competitors, technology capabilities, and external benchmarks.

Unified Accountability: A key reason why companies like Amazon, Zoom, and the aforementioned local Cincinnati wine retailer are nimble is that they have been able to place limits on internal organizational silos. Amazon could not possibly have hired hundreds of thousands of people, added a ton of new delivery infrastructure, and introduced new IT capabilities during the pandemic had human resources, supply chain, IT, and finance been unable to move together rapidly as one unit. The challenge, especially for large organizations, arises when the goals for one function (e.g., managing capital investments for the finance function) become misaligned with those of another function (e.g., the need to rapidly buy more delivery vehicles during the pandemic). To be clear, functional organizations within the company play vital performance, efficiency, and compliance roles. You do want finance to strictly manage capital investments and supply chain to ensure high delivery service levels. The challenge is to optimize decisions that must cross functional silos. That's where the principle of *Unified Accountability* comes in. That principle drives clarity of ownership for end-to-end business process outcomes. It prioritizes overall business results over siloed considerations.

To be clear, functional organizations do have their merits. They are established structures, and their procedures, standards, and measures have been developed over decades. They exist because they are very effective, especially in stable environments. However, there is a downside when it comes to end-to-end business process optimization. Siloed business processes within companies inevitably slow things down and fall out-of-sync as the business grows and becomes more complex. The trade-off between speed and scale of business processes is a well-known phenomenon. It needs to be approached with finesse. For instance, you cannot just sweep up all functions (finance, IT, supply chain, etc.) under one owner and assume that the silo problem has been solved. Detailed cross-functional business processes must be re-designed at a very granular level.

Another known trade-off relates to innovativeness versus stable structure. It's important to acknowledge that this is an inherent paradox for large-scale business processes. Dynamic business processes require ideas to germinate from all parts of the organization (as in "let a thousand flowers bloom"). However, stable processes require a deliberate structure and defined standards. In our experience, this trade-off is better managed when the organization has a clear single owner for a given end-to-end business process.

These two paradoxical issues—speed versus scale, and innovation versus stability—point to why a *Unified Accountability* model is required. It does address and reconcile them.

Dynamic Operating Engine: Let's assume that an organization is good at setting the right business goals driven by *Open Market Rules* and also avoids siloed behavior via *Unified Accountability*. It faces one final business process adaptability challenge before it can deliver sustained operational excellence: it needs an operating model that enables its people to consistently translate strategy into action. Functions like finance and HR have fragmented and evolved origins, and unsurprisingly, most companies have a multitude of operating styles. The ways in which daily operations, continual improvement, financial costing of processes, and so on are conducted can vary. Without a consistent operating model, driving constant change is hard. The only way to resolve this is via a methodology that converts the constantly changing business process goals into consistent and repeatable day-to-day employee actions that together deliver excellence in execution. This is what we refer to as the *Dynamic Operating Engine*.

Additionally, this operating engine binds together the people who may have come from siloed functions (finance, supply chain, IT, HR, etc.), as well as different tools and capabilities, into a culture of "one-team, one-dream." It codifies approaches to dynamic business processes evolution, besides generating an agile employee culture of swift responsiveness and proactivity. In this way, it ensures that the business operations change dynamically over time, without the need for episodic jolts of course correction.

To illustrate how these three drivers—*Open Market Rules*, *Unified Accountability*, and *Dynamic Operating Engine*—can come together to form a lasting set of dynamic business processes, we examine Procter & Gamble's market-beating performance under A.G. Lafley, one of the most lauded CEOs in corporate history.[3]

Procter & Gamble's Restructuring Program

Early in the year 2000, P&G was in real trouble. In the preceding years, there had been a realization within the company that it needed to restructure.[4] Revenue growth, which had varied between 1.4% and 5.5% between 1995 and 1999, was well below P&G's internal target of 7%. Earnings per share (EPS) had fallen well below the goal of 14% to 15%. The organization design of the previous decades had gone stale and become a bottleneck to growth. At the end of 1998, a six-year corporate restructure program, futuristically called *Organization 2005*, was announced. It would substantially redesign the company's structure, work processes, and culture.

The trigger for change was this restructure program, and its effects would be long-lasting. A.G. Lafley took over the company in June 2000 to complete that restructure. Within the next ten years, it had more than doubled its sales and market capitalization, making it one of the five most valuable companies in the United States and among the ten most valuable companies in the world. What happened during that period is highly instructive for our model of *Dynamic Process Transformation*. Underpinning this sustained business performance was a finely choreographed dynamic business process transformation in which every function and business unit—and, ultimately, every employee—"played their position."[5]

How Procter & Gamble Organized for Dynamic Business Operations

The concept of *Dynamic Process Transformation* drivers did not exist at the time, so it's fascinating to see how completely the strategies adopted by P&G fit this new model. Let's illustrate how the specific actions taken would fit each of the three drivers.

Open Market Rules: The principle driving the organization design was simple. Each of the company's three main activities—product lines, local country sales, and business process operations—had to be organized to compete directly in the open market. That meant that the company's structure, as well as its performance metrics, had to be set up along these three axes:

- Global Business Units (GBUs): P&G moved from four geographical business units to seven GBUs based on global product lines. That put the responsibility for strategy and profit on the brands.

- Market Development Organizations (MDOs): P&G established eight MDO regions with the objective of tailoring global sales and marketing programs to compete effectively in local markets.

- Global Business Services (GBS): Operational functions such as human resources, accounting, order management, procurement, and information technology were consolidated from separate geographic regions into one corporate organization. The $2.5Bn Global Business Services organization would later be led by co-author Filippo Passerini.

For each of these three organizations, the open market performance rules were very clear. GBUs had to deliver top-tier performance within their industries. MDOs had to add about two additional percentage points of growth. GBS had to deliver effective and efficient process operations. Additionally, a thin layer of Corporate Function organizations (HR, IT, finance, etc.) was retained, for compliance, governance, and capability building within their respective areas.

Each one of these organizations had to win in their respective "markets," based solely on the success measures of their "customers" (i.e., the consumer, the retail clients, and the internal employees / business operations respectively for GBUs, MDOs and GBS).

Unified Accountability: The three-axis matrix organization structure facilitated unified accountability, thus delivering a sustained decade of unprecedented company performance.

Here's how *Unified Accountability* became a force multiplier to operations. Under P&G's previous structure, siloed organizations and reward systems hindered growth. Regional and local country businesses had profit and operating power. The result was entrenched geographic silos that prevented strong products like Cover Girl, which had been acquired earlier, from being globally deployed for about a decade.

The old matrixed structure also created silos among the global functions. Thus, for instance, while Supply Chain made strides in improving manufacturing costs and reliability, R&D's reward system favored developing premium-price products, despite consumers becoming increasingly price sensitive.

Under the new design, the restructure program delivered clear and unified accountability for business outcomes. Complete accountability for products (e.g., Laundry) now rested with the GBUs. Full accountability for country or regional issues (e.g., local selling, talent and compliance issues, and minor changes to marketing and products) resided with the MDOs. And unified accountability for internal business services (e.g., common services ranging from accounting to HR to order management) resided with GBS.

Each one of these organizations was responsible for its respective goals and objectives, end-to-end; at the same time, their interdependency was clear to all.

Dynamic Operating Engine: Every operating unit—whether a GBU, an MDO, GBS, or Corporate Functions—developed operating models in line with the newly designed corporate structure. It's best to illustrate this with the example of GBS.

The context of GBS was somewhat unique. This organization simply did not exist prior to the restructure. Initially, it was carved out from various functions (HR, finance, etc.) or geographies (US, Germany, etc.). At the start, there wasn't an operating model for GBS to work as a single unit. As a result, in its initial days, GBS was more of a federated collection of functional service leaders. That changed within the first year. Driven by the mission to deliver competitive costs and functional services, GBS set up offshore service centers in Costa Rica, Manila, and Newcastle. As work started to move from historical geographic offices to the service-center back offices, an operating model began to emerge. GBS could be reimagined as if it were an internal services company. It could take in service requests from P&G business units (e.g., monthly closing of financial books, or employee payroll, or email services) and then decide how to scale this work, optimize it, and deliver it via the three service centers in Costa Rica, Manila, and Newcastle.

In other words, the employees within GBS changed from working for a function (e.g., HR or finance) to working in the business process services industry (e.g., payroll services industry or financial closing services industry). That was a subtle but powerful shift. The *Dynamic Operating Engine* in the latter empowers you to work across functional silos, geographic boundaries, different sourcing options, and disparate solutions, with a goal of delivering an efficient, effective, and value-creating "product/service." So, for instance, a person who had always run payroll operations could now think of themselves as if they were virtually the CEO of a payroll services company. The difference in mindset, accountability, and ability to innovate was significant.

Over time, this came to be referred to as "running GBS as a business." This approach was directly responsible for delivering best-in-class results consistently and for P&G's GBS being recognized as #1 in the industry. P&G incorporated into the GBS *Dynamic Operating Engine* all the practices expected in a regular business, such as account management with internal P&G business unit clients, annual service product strategy (e.g., annual payroll service strategy), benchmarking, disruptive innovation, and service product pricing, as well as a clear and ever-evolving value proposition for all "GBS products."

This model fueled a positive spiral of transparency between internal process operations and the business, as well as value creation through cost reduction, improved service quality, and new business-building capabilities.

The Effect of Dynamic Business Operations on P&G Business Results

The cumulative effect of every new P&G organizational unit playing to peak performance was to deliver consistent and sustainable competitive advantage. With Lafley leading the company throughout the 2000s, P&G more than doubled sales. During that time, the company's portfolio of billion-dollar brands grew from 10 to 24 (including former brands Folgers and Actonel), and the number of brands with sales between $500 million and $1 billion increased fivefold. Interestingly, the business top line and profit growth in the P&G beauty segment exceeded that of a Wall Street darling at the time—Apple—for the same period.

As this example makes clear, the drivers of *Dynamic Process Transformation* are extremely powerful. How to go about applying this model in a step-by-step fashion will be the focus of the rest of the book. The question for most business leaders today is not whether we should be consumer oriented, externally focused, or innovative. All three, it goes without saying, are inherent in our jobs. The question, rather, is how a company's people can go about transforming an operating model to support a business model within their unique situation. We need a road map to help translate key objectives into execution. That's where the *Dynamic Process Transformation* model, described in the remaining chapters, comes in.

How to Read This Book

This book was designed for business executives who are seeking sustained competitive advantage for their organizations.

In an ever-changing world, the desire to implement a successful process transformation and/or digital transformation is valid. If executed successfully, it will help the business succeed in the near term. Therein lies the issue. The world continues to change even after your transformation program has been executed. This book is for strategic leaders who understand this; they want to build operations that will last. As change cycles accelerate, the efficacy period of one-off business process transformations gets shorter and shorter. Strategic leaders demand a more enduring competitive advantage.

This book sets up a road map that will enable you to lead your organization into sustained and ongoing transformation. It will also provide you with tangible steps and tips based on the authors having executed this successfully in a Fortune 20 company. Part 1 of the book covers the *Dynamic Process Transformation* model and what types of issues it can address. Chapter 1 introduces a road map based on a four-stage model of maturity for dynamic business process transformation. The good news for bold change leaders is that there is an optimal path to getting to dynamic business processes. It involves accelerating the journey across the four stages of maturity. Chapter 1 will describe those stages and how to move from one to the next.

Chapter 2 starts with the dilemmas facing all leaders in business process transformation by telling three stories. For most leaders, the outcomes of transformation seem to be constantly moving as the business evolves. Change resistance is natural, but make no mistake, that resistance must be overcome. Automation and technology become outdated almost before they are implemented, and thus the choices made are extremely consequential. As a result of all these challenges, by the time the transformation program is complete, it seems as if the landscape has changed again. Chapter 2 frames the issues that the *Dynamic Process Transformation* model seeks to address.

Parts II to V detail the four stages of maturity for dynamic processes. Each stage of maturity has three chapters that dig deep into the three drivers—*Open Market Rules, Unified Accountability,* and *Dynamic Operating Engine* respectively. This is intended to provide a playbook for all actions you will need to take as you move from one stage of maturity to the next.

Finally, Part VI on *Achieving Competitive Advantage via Business Operations* provides a plan of action. It presents the opportunity for the current generation of process transformation leaders to create a successful legacy for their people and their businesses.

The next chapter introduces the four-stage *Dynamic Process Transformation* model and outlines how leaders can follow a proven path to accelerating their transformation journey.

PART I

How Business Processes Become a Competitive Disadvantage

The *Dynamic Process Transformation* Model (4x3 matrix)

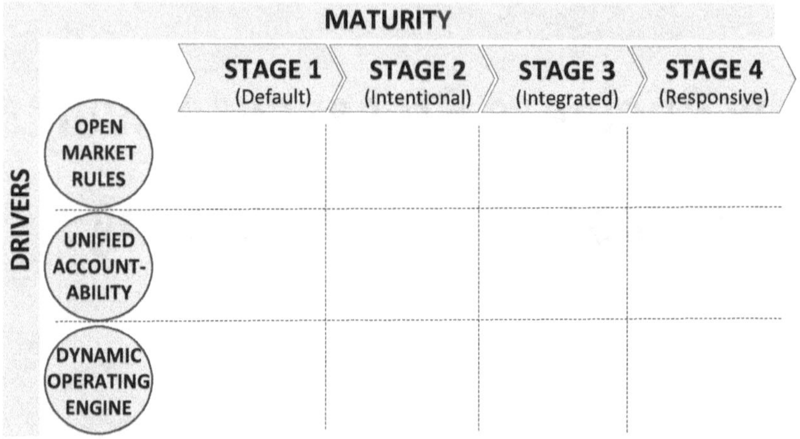

	MATURITY			
DRIVERS	STAGE 1 (Default)	STAGE 2 (Intentional)	STAGE 3 (Integrated)	STAGE 4 (Responsive)
OPEN MARKET RULES				
UNIFIED ACCOUNT-ABILITY				
DYNAMIC OPERATING ENGINE				

What is the *Dynamic Process Transformation* 4x3 Matrix?

The 4x3 matrix lays out the interplay between the maturity levels and the drivers of process transformation. The drivers take the organization from one maturity level to the next. The drivers also help tailor the strategies and action steps for changing maturity levels.

Actions to increase maturity from starting point to end point

- UNDERSTAND the current maturity level of business processes.

- TARGET the end stage maturity level.

- BUILD specific action plans based on the three drivers.

FIGURE 2: *Dynamic Process Transformation* Model

1

Introducing the *Dynamic Process Transformation* Model

KEY INSIGHT: Recognizing that you have a dynamic process problem is half the battle.

Filippo's Story

As I (Filippo) drove home from the Procter & Gamble HQ in downtown Cincinnati one evening in May 2003, I wondered why I wasn't feeling happier. After all, that day marked the successful conclusion of a particularly difficult chapter in P&G's effort to outsource part of its functional back-office operations. It had been a few years of organizational turmoil. First there was the aborted effort to sell functional services like IT, finance, and HR as a service to other multinationals. Next came the unsuccessful outsourcing of 6,000 employees to Electronic Data Services (EDS). All this uncertainty had been rough on the organization.

I had recently been brought in to drive closure, and we devised a new plan: to outsource two-thirds of the back-office operations to three separate services companies. Today, we had finally announced the largest of the three deals, this one with Hewlett-Packard Services. P&G and HP Services had revealed, earlier in the day, a ten-year $3Bn deal, wherein about 2,000 P&G employees across more than 70 countries would transfer to HP. It was hailed as the largest and best structured and executed Global Business Services outsourcing deal in the world.

I had recently taken on the role of Global Business Services (GBS) leader of P&G. The aforementioned aborted GBS projects had created significant turmoil. My first task in the new role had been to end that turmoil by developing a new strategy and successfully completing the outsourcing deals. Today marked the completion of the first major milestone. Except that something still bothered me.

The Landscape of P&G's Functional Back-Office Operations

It might help for me to describe the context of this issue first. All companies have functional organizations like finance, sales, HR, IT, procurement, supply chain, and so on. They are the back-office backbone of the day-to-day business processes that deliver the company's operations. P&G's strong functions had historically helped it become a global powerhouse. The company restructure program, mentioned in the previous chapter, had taken that up a notch. By sweeping together the operational parts of all these functions into Global Business Services (GBS), we aimed to achieve even more efficiency.

In general, GBS groups focus on running many routine functional administrative tasks, leaving the business units more time to focus on customer or product-specific activities.[6] GBS organizations deliver shared transactional services, such as managing orders or payroll to all the subsidiaries of the company. Thus, the term Global Shared Services, or alternatively, Global Business Services. P&G had in fact coined the term GBS.

So far this might seem like a rosy picture of P&G's GBS. It is, except for the fact that earlier in the chapter I mentioned the intention to outsource most of it. It is legitimate to ask why a company might want to outsource such a great asset.

The Early Success of P&G's GBS

My predecessor in the company, Mike Power, deserves credit for having pushed to create a GBS organization and to lead its initial phase.

The first cost reduction benefits of the previously mentioned corporate restructure, which involved creating offshore service centers in Manila, Costa Rica, and Newcastle, were delivered under Power's leadership. P&G's GBS was a pioneer in many of these activities. Indeed, this is what convinced the government of Costa Rica to enter the shared services industry, a decision that would over time lead this industry to be among Costa Rica's top economic drivers.

The new GBS operation, with its offshore centers, was an external success story that drew envy, and inquiries. Other multinational companies expressed interest in buying functional services (such as IT or finance) from P&G's GBS. That led to the idea that perhaps the new organization could "monetize" itself by selling its services to others.

P&G's GBS Goes on Sale

However, the idea of monetizing GBS further by selling its services to other companies quickly fell out of favor, since selling functional services was not core to P&G's mission. It would be a distraction for a consumer goods company to enter that business. Over time, an alternative idea emerged. If P&G's functional operations could be run in offshore countries, and if GBS operations were not core to P&G's business, and furthermore, if GBS was in fact a monetizable asset, then perhaps it would be better to sell or outsource all of GBS to a services provider.

That led to the second project: to outsource all 6,000 GBS employees to a single provider.

It is hard for me to overstate just how much of a cultural change that decision was for P&G at the time. The company had historically been a lifetime employer. People started at the entry level and spent their entire career in the company, often leading to their children and grandchildren following in their footsteps. It was hard to imagine being outsourced to a supplier company, because it meant, in effect, moving to a new employer.

This project almost went through, with EDS being the chosen supplier. However, in a strange twist of fate, the deal fell through literally hours before being signed. EDS's stock price fell dramatically that day for unrelated reasons, which made the sale price unviable. That was just as well, because there had been unease at the idea of selling the entire GBS organization to a single supplier.

That is the point where I took up the Global GBS leader role. The GBS organization felt a bit battered by the twists and turns of the previous years, and it was important for the company to drive all this to closure. Probably a better idea would be to selectively outsource to a few suppliers, each of them best-of-breed in their respective functions. In other words, utilize a combination of the three best providers in IT services, HR services, and facilities services. It was very important to quickly execute this and to drive this uncertain era to a successful close.

My Dilemma Becomes Clearer

This final plan was executed on a war footing. I will not elaborate on the selection of the best-of-breed suppliers, as it is not important for this book, which is about process transformation. By the time the dust settled six months later, we had selected HP for IT services, IBM for HR services, and Jones Lang Lasalle for facilities management services.

On the day in May 2003 that we selected HP, I had a feeling of unease as I drove home from the office. That was the largest and most complex of the outsourcing deals, and it marked the end of a prolonged period of uncertainty.

As I parked my car at home and sat there in silence for a few moments, I finally realized why I wasn't feeling happier. Perhaps these outsourcing deals were solutions to a symptom, not to a root cause. The root of the issue was simple—the functional operations that comprised GBS were not unique to P&G's business. The journey from GBS being viewed as a global competitive advantage four years earlier, to being thought of as nonstrategic, had been brutally short. It seemed to me at the time that my predecessors had taken all the right steps in the GBS journey to centralize and standardize operations and to reduce costs via offshore centers. Yet if GBS was not distinctive to P&G business operations, that meant it was fundamentally a commodity. Therefore, nothing prevented our future from being a series of painful outsourcing deals until there was nothing left of GBS. And given the unique capabilities that GBS could bring to the business, was this the best outcome for P&G? If not, what could we do to change that?

Analyzing My Dilemma Eventually Leads to the Idea for *Dynamic Process Transformation*

I did not at that point have a good answer to my dilemma, and I wouldn't fully develop one for some time. In fact, as I reflect today on my statement of the dilemma, it strikes me that it was too narrowly focused on GBS. The issue was actually bigger than GBS.

The strategic question was whether P&G's business processes were fully optimized at the end of this episode of outsourcing. Or was outsourcing just one step in an ongoing journey to achieve enduring competitive advantage via *Dynamic Process Transformation*?

Perhaps my question should have been—were the business processes that were run by P&G's GBS, including those which were now operated via outsourcing, so good that they could not be transformed further? In today's world, in which the capacity of digital technology to keep transforming even efficient operations is recognized, this might seem like a silly question. Yet that question is still worth asking today.

The Need for a *Dynamic Process Transformation* Model

There is a basic dilemma around business process transformation that most leaders confront. They absolutely want their operations to become more adaptable and more strategic; that's not the question. It's just that the path from "good" to "great" is unknown, and the costs and benefits unclear. Examples that describe the flexibility of Silicon Valley company operations tend not to be useful because those operations were designed from scratch. The challenge for companies that carry legacy business processes is very different. The question is not so much whether a company *should* transform its business processes for ongoing business value, but whether it is *able* to, and *how*. We need a road map to execute *Dynamic Process Transformation* that begins from a complex and muddy starting point and that delivers predictable outcomes.

The Model for *Dynamic Process Transformation*

All organizations fall somewhere along a defined spectrum of maturity of business processes. This spectrum can be divided into four distinct stages of maturity ranging from Stage 1—*default business processes*, through to Stage 4—*responsive business processes*. It follows that we need to pinpoint our start and end points on this spectrum. Therein lies the first problem. In this evolving industry of business process transformation, there isn't a reliable way to measure our start and end points. We will address this via the four stages in the *Dynamic Process Transformation* model.

Next, we need to know which levers to pull to travel from the starting to the ending maturity stage. We refer to these levers as the *drivers* of dynamic business processes. They are the same three drivers—*Open Market Rules, Unified Accountability*, and *Dynamic Operating Engine*—that were introduced in the previous chapter.

The four stages of maturity help us measure progress from current to future state, while the drivers specify the levers you pull to make progress. The combination of the two provides a road map for evolution to *Dynamic Process Transformation*. Figure 2, provided at the beginning of Part 1 of this book, lays out the model in a matrix format with the three drivers as rows and the four maturity stages as columns. At each of the four stages of maturity, there are specific actions that need to be taken for each of the three drivers. The 4x3 matrix lays out what needs to change in the business process design if organizations are to evolve in maturity. Those four stages of maturity are described in the following paragraphs; the individual cells in the 4x3 matrix will be expanded on in the remainder of the book.

The Four Stages of Maturity of Business Processes

The good news for leaders looking for a road map to dynamic business processes is that each of the four stages of maturity has distinct characteristics. Moreover, there are clear steps that can take our organization up the maturity levels.

STAGE 1: Default Business Processes

Every business has business processes, whether deliberately designed or not. And all businesses measure the performance of their business processes. For instance, every organization measures its sales, profits, payroll, orders, and so on. Key performance indicators within finance, sales, marketing, supply chain, information technology, and others, foster predictable outcomes at appropriate costs. This is the starting point for all organizations—that is, measuring key performance indicators of key business processes and holding functional leaders accountable for delivering those metrics. As the saying goes, you get what you measure.

The Stage 1 (default) of the *Dynamic Process Transformation* model acknowledges this starting point. During Stage 1, the organization benefits by standardizing, stabilizing, and measuring functional performance for ongoing improvement. Many organizations view this as an acceptable long-term stage. If the business strategy demands that every ounce of available focus be placed externally, and if there is no disruptive threat on the horizon, then this may just be a good enough stage for the moment. It may also be fine for businesses whose products and services have demand inelasticity. If greater process effectiveness doesn't impact market share significantly, then Stage 1 maturity is a good enough parking spot.

STAGE 2: Intentional Business Processes

Over time, the inevitable demands of productivity and performance will require you to be more deliberate about improving business processes. Customer orders that require manual labor for their processing may be fine when the business is small, but automation becomes inevitable as that business grows. Similarly, having one system for employee time sheets managed by HR, and running a totally different system managed by finance to deliver the resulting pay slips, may be fine up to a point, but the calls for "connection" between these two business processes will get louder as the workforce grows. At Stage 2, there must be close collaboration, and deliberate streamlining and automation, across functional silos. The need for greater productivity and employee effectiveness demands it. However, at Stage 2, the ownership of work may still reside within the respective functions—within HR, finance, procurement, sales, and so on.

Interestingly, most companies fall into this stage. Multinational companies may have a patchwork of different business processes and IT systems that either evolved within various countries or were introduced through company acquisitions. The challenge for these organizations is to standardize business processes across different units. To deliver the next level of performance, these processes must evolve from fragmented to standard systems. This is often done via a series of arduous, expensive, and episodic transformations, made even more unpalatable by the 70% failure rate of transformation projects.

Stage 2 is characterized by intentional designs to overcome challenges like the above. There is also a growing focus on driving continuous improvement and productivity. And, although business processes are still managed by their respective functions, there is good collaboration to improve business processes end-to-end.

STAGE 3: Integrated Business Processes

The prior stage, *Intentional Business Processes*, is sufficient to support the efficiency needs of even large corporations for a while. What eventually breaks the dam on Stage 2 is the need for significantly improved cross-functional efficiency and effectiveness. At Stage 3 the functional silo structure must be broken. The trigger for change could be proactive or reactive. Perhaps functional budgets have been cut to the bone and cannot be reduced further within each functional silo. Or perhaps the business wants to pursue a lean operation as part of its corporate strategy (e.g., Everyday Low Price at Walmart). Whatever the immediate cause, we must make our operations leaner and more responsive. A small percentage of professionally managed companies, operating near the top of their industry ranks, currently perform at this stage.

Although not strictly necessary, most companies at this stage of maturity have some type of GBS structure. That structure helps eliminate functional silos by managing business processes across them. GBS structures can also help establish accountability for end-to-end business process outcomes. So, for instance, consider the Stage 2 siloed structure of having order management done by the sales function, delivery of products run by the supply chain, and cash receivables operated by finance. Creating an end-to-end business process of "order-to-cash" within GBS optimizes work across all three functional silos. Today, end-to-end process management such as procure-to-pay, hire-to-retire, concept-to-product, deployment-to-retrograde, market-to-prospect, molecule-to-shelf, and so on, have become de facto best practices for mature GBS operations. The existence of a GBS leader, one who can help design these processes without the influence of historical boundaries of functional silos, is a huge enabler. Structures like GBS can help integrate and stitch together business processes across historical boundaries.

STAGE 4: Responsive Business Processes

The major difference between the *Integrated Business Processes* of a Stage 3 and the *Responsive Business Processes* of a Stage 4 has to do with adaptability to change. The ability to organically evolve business processes in response to customer, economic, competitive, and similar factors makes this stage a truly worthwhile goal.

At Stage 4, your internal operations become your ongoing competitive advantage. Amazon.com, with its advantage in automation and analytics in online selling, its superiority in warehousing and transportation, and its relentless pursuit of ongoing efficiency, is a prime example, to use a bad pun. At Stage 4, business processes aren't just enabling the business, they are creating new business possibilities. This requires leadership mindsets and skills, in addition to operational excellence.

Stage 4 delivers more than just streamlined and dynamic operations. It also fosters "living" transformation, which sets up an ongoing spiral of speed, efficiency, and effectiveness. It addresses the biggest challenge faced by business operations, which is to ensure that business processes do not become obsolete over time.

These four stages of maturity, along with the three drivers of change mentioned in the previous chapter, provide the map of *Dynamic Process Transformation*. But as with any map, the real work is in the actions of going from one point to another. Part 2 of this book will begin to address that. However, even before that, there is a first step: deciding whether to make the journey. We return to Filippo's story to examine his realization that P&G needed to embark on that odyssey.

Filippo's Story, Continued:
What I Did Not Realize in May 2003

As I drove home that evening in May 2003, I had started to realize that P&G's business processes needed to keep transforming over time and that the GBS organization could perhaps be an important lever for the company along that path. In hindsight, the P&G GBS of 2003, which included outsourcing some services, was at Stage 2 of maturity. What I did not yet realize was that this spectrum had four stages and that over time we would discover the secret sauce to moving the organization through those stages. I had no way of knowing that over the next several years the P&G GBS organization would play a leadership role in this. I couldn't predict that it would soon be considered the best in the world in its lane, be awarded multiple times by the industry, and be the subject of case studies in the *Harvard Business Review*. There was no inkling that information technology would drive the fourth industrial revolution and that organizations such as GBS were uniquely positioned to put together three key ingredients: enabling technologies, process management expertise, and transformation management skills. I did not yet understand the potential of dynamic business processes or that we would be constructing a road map of how to achieve them reliably. However, I had identified the dilemma facing us, and that was a major step toward making the rest of the journey.

Driving Dynamic Business Processes by Using GBS

I learned over time that the GBS framework offered a way to deliver dynamic business transformation. Fast-forward to today, the GBS construct has matured into a full industry. The role of GBS as a leader in transforming processes is generally accepted. This is based on a strong foundation of results. GBS organizations, when set up correctly, deliver annual productivity savings of greater than 15%.[7] More than 9 out of 10 enterprises, across all industries and company dimensions, use shared services already.[8] In most large and medium-sized organizations, the GBS scope of work cuts across almost all, if not all, functions.[9] The GBS global market size is currently $110Bn[10] and growing at a compound annual growth rate (CAGR) of 17%.

Next, combine this potent GBS construct with a codified model for building *Dynamic Process Transformation*, and things get even more interesting! The codified *Dynamic Process Transformation* model is a big deal. That's because there is strong consistency across functional business processes between industries. Processing a payment follows a similar course whether done at Walmart or at Tencent or by the French government. Between the proven GBS construct and the codified *Dynamic Process Transformation* model, the opportunity for creating enduring competitive advantage is virtually limitless.

Is GBS the Only Model to Drive This Evolution?

At this point it may be fair to ask about the linkage between the GBS organization structure and dynamic business processes. Is a GBS organization structure essential? After all, the examples of Amazon, Zoom, and the Cincinnati wine store don't involve a P&G GBS-like structure.

I want to be crystal clear on this: Dynamic business processes don't necessarily require a GBS structure. However, for medium to large companies that start out with legacy functional structures (as opposed to being digitally native), GBS can be a huge enabler. There are only three ingredients needed for dynamic business processes: the three drivers of *Open Market Rules, Unified Accountability*, and *Dynamic Operating Engine*. A highly mature GBS organization will operate on *Open Market Rules*. It will be organized for *Unified Accountability* of end-to-end business processes. And it will run its day-to-day operations using a methodology based on the *Dynamic Operating Engine*. So yes, in the right context, a strong GBS organization or a GBS-like structure can accelerate the delivery of dynamic business processes. But make no mistake, organizational structures don't deliver business outcomes by themselves. At best, they facilitate them.

The rest of the book describes how to go about designing and delivering the road map to dynamic business processes. But first, we must better understand what problems must be solved as an organization sets out to embrace dynamic business processes. For that, see the next chapter.

2

Dilemmas Facing Leaders
on Business Process Transformation

> **KEY INSIGHT:** There is an optimal mix of the three drivers for you to move from one stage of maturity to the next.

Congratulations on having made it to Chapter 2! We jest, of course. It's not that we presume to lose readers at this point. However, we do assume that your continued interest implies some intent to put into *practice* the concepts so far presented. That's important, because in the words of Yogi Berra, the American baseball player and cultural icon, whose amusing "Yogi-isms" often incorporate common wisdom, "In theory, there is no difference between theory and practice. But in practice, there is." Or, as Thomas Edison put it dryly, "Vision without execution is hallucination." As practitioners with a combined seven decades of experience in dynamic business process transformation, we wholeheartedly agree. Therefore, we have designed this book to serve as a *practical* road map.

So then, how should we put the concepts from the previous chapter into practice? In that chapter we mentioned that we start by using the maturity stages to lock in our current state and our future target. We then use the drivers to create the sequence of action steps needed to progress to the future state. Having said that, real life is hardly ever straightforward.

New and unexpected challenges arise over time. Then there's the fact that the three drivers interact and rely upon one another to be effective. And there are intermediate goals for maturity development along the way—the crawl–walk–run stages, as it were. Let's illustrate how this happens using a real-life model. During early childhood, as a baby progresses from crawling to walking to running (i.e., maturity levels in our case), multiple skills (i.e., drivers in our book) come into play. For instance, a baby needs a sense of their body in space, as in where their limbs are relative to the floor (i.e., vestibular sense). Then there are the muscular skills to propel the body (i.e., motor sense). And then there's brain development, to translate intent into action (i.e., neurological sense). These three skills/drivers are distinct, but they work together. Some mix of the three is necessary for each stage in the baby's development from crawling to walking to running. Every child's development path is different, but the three skills and three stages of maturity are a common framework.

That's how we intend our three drivers and four maturity levels to relate to one another. A *Dynamic Process Transformation* will need a mix of all three drivers—*Open Market Rules, Unified Accountability*, and *Dynamic Operating Engine*—to progress up the four levels of maturity.

To isolate and illustrate the specific effects of each driver, this chapter will introduce three real-life case studies—one per driver. We start with the first driver: *Open Market Rules*.

Driver #1. *Open Market Rules*:
A Fortune 500 CIO Transforms IT from Function to Service-Centricity

Francisco Fraga, currently Senior Vice President and Chief Information Officer of US Pharmaceutical at McKesson, is a rare breed of IT leader. He's a technologist who's a business leader at heart. He has run best-in-class IT operations for a Fortune 20 company but is an innovator underneath it all. Over a career spanning 27 years around the world, he's created several global success stories. However, he considers a fundamental transformation of the IT function that he led at a $10Bn Fortune 500 global foods and beverages company to be his greatest success so far.

When Francisco took over as Chief Technology and Information Officer, the company required him to deliver significantly improved IT costs and reliability. After several years of robust stock price growth, recent months had witnessed significant stock decline. Acquisitions and divestitures put further pressure on business processes. Within three months of his joining the company, the stock had tanked to the point that there was chatter on Wall Street about the shrinking financials drawing activist investors. It was a daunting situation for any new leader. Strong demands to reduce costs and improve service levels were developing at the same time as a huge new workload related to restructure. The targets were daunting. Yet by the time Francisco left the company four and a half years later, its IT function was widely viewed as equal to or better than industry benchmarks.

Francisco's Approach:
An Open Market IT Organization

When Francisco took over the organization, IT was divided into IT applications, IT infrastructure, and cybersecurity, with a couple of IT leaders as client managers for business units. But at the same time, the company itself was functionally oriented—that is, organized in terms of finance, supply chain, HR, and so on. For context, most large global companies tend to be either function-centric or business-unit-centric, with some underlying matrix structure to harmonize between the two. The fact that in Francisco's company IT had been neither function-centric nor business-unit-centric may seem odd, but it is not uncommon. For reasons of scale, many IT organizations are structured into IT applications, infrastructure, cybersecurity, and so on. You achieve lower costs and better service levels if you group common work. Hopefully. We say "hopefully" because this structure comes with its silos. This can create silos within IT, silos within internal business processes, and definitely silos related to the external customer of the business.

Francisco's choice was to reverse all of this by moving the organization from internal silo oriented to *Open Market Rules* oriented.

Step 1 for Francisco was to reorganize IT along the company's functional value streams—that is, supply chain, R&D, sales, marketing, human resources, and finance. There were also some enabling functions within IT to support the above (cybersecurity, IT infrastructure, data & analytics, etc.). The transformation was significant. First, his leaders had to transition from being focused on technical deliverables such as IT infrastructure or applications, to focusing on business value (e.g., excellent supply chain performance). Second, their role was expanded to include all aspects of these new services (i.e., to deliver day-to-day services and continuous improvement as well as long-term disruptive innovation). Their roles would be akin to those of any product or brand manager in a product company. For example, just as a product manager for the Apple iPhone is held accountable for everything ranging from product design to product supply, competition, and long-term strategy, the IT supply chain services manager would be completely accountable for the service's quality, cost of ownership, and value contribution. Francisco called this role a *service manager* role, rather than a product manager role, since the context here was related to services. And finally, the service manager role included external benchmarking goals. This meant improved cost tracking and, in some cases, outsourcing the work to third-party suppliers if they provided better value. These changes oriented his organization toward playing by *Open Market Rules*. For all intents and purposes, these service managers had to operate as if they were small independent companies in an open market.

Step 2 was to redesign the internal IT operational processes and to strategically leverage external service providers. That strengthened internal process discipline, improved agility to respond to business opportunities with speed, and focused the organization on business outcomes rather than on internal key performance indicators (KPIs) and siloed execution.

Finally, Step 3 was to develop service management skills throughout the IT organization. Francisco started by training the leaders of the organization; he also ensured that the new service management skills stuck by building them bottom-up. That is, his strategy for the organization was a two-way road.

The results were dramatic. Within a couple of years of introducing this structure, Francisco and his team hit all their goals of delivering distinctive meaningful business value, higher service quality, and reduced costs as a percentage of revenue. There were operational improvements (e.g., IT operating costs were reduced meaningfully, organization satisfaction soared as the total number of IT incidents was reduced by 60%) and business value creation jumped. Within a few years, the IT organization was being entrusted to drive major cross-functional transformation programs in the company, such as the Integrated Business Planning Transformation.

What Challenges Had to Be Overcome?

Francisco's journey was anything but easy—he faced many hurdles. For example, he had to identify and execute solutions to the following questions:

- How to evolve functional-efficiency-based "default KPIs" into more business-centric ones.

- How to create more end-to-end (E2E) global process owner structures that aligned better with business outcomes.

- How to ensure that all transformation projects were business-value-centric.

- How to drive an open market mindset within the organization.

Francisco's chosen approach to restructuring his organization for service-centricity solved these challenges elegantly. He rapidly grasped the business context. He then framed a plan to create a dynamic *Open Market Rules* organization to deliver the win.

We now move to our second driver—*Unified Accountability*—to bring to life another remarkable story.

Driver #2. *Unified Accountability:*
A Fortune 5 Company Goes from Good to Great on Accounts Payable
after Implementing End-to-End Accountability

Yazdi Bagli, Executive Vice President of Enterprise Business Services at Kaiser Permanente, is likely the world's foremost practitioner of business process optimization. Over more than three decades, he has helped some of the biggest companies in the world transform their business processes and operations. Yazdi considers his most memorable business process transformation to be the one that dramatically improved accounts payables at a Fortune 5 company.

In 2018, Yazdi assumed the Enterprise Business Services (or GBS) leader role at a Fortune 5 retailer. In the highly competitive retail industry, operating costs spell the difference between market leadership and bankruptcy. In this context, the role of the Enterprise Business Services leader is crucial, not just for reliable and cost-effective operations but also in developing new and innovative ways to stay a step ahead of the competition. In retail operations, accounts payables is key. Besides affecting cycle times and operating costs, it can provide a competitive edge if suppliers prefer to work with the retailer, thus enhancing negotiation leverage.

Is Our Operation Good Enough, or Is It as Good as It Can Be?

In this instance, Yazdi found that the accounts payables process seemed fine on the surface. The service operations metrics such as days to pay, cost per invoice, number of wrong payments made, and so on were robust. The cost of operating the entire payables shared service was also comparable with the standard for the industry. So the accounts payables process was just fine, when viewed from this high-level benchmarking perspective. Yazdi, however, had a different question for himself: Was the accounts payable process good enough, or was it as good as it could be? His organization had more than 1,000 people supporting this process. That was easy to rationalize, given the size of the Fortune 5 company, but the question against that was, "If we are that big, shouldn't we see a higher-scale advantage than others?" The presence of 1,000 accounts payables staff indicated that the company's GBS could possibly be better.

Yazdi's Approach:
Unified Accountability to Reduce Defects on Accounts Payables

Over the years, Yazdi has developed his own approach to improving process operations based on the Theory of Constraints (TOC).[11] The big idea behind TOC is that every process has a constraint (bottleneck). The fastest and most effective path to improved throughput is to focus your efforts on that constraint. Yazdi's first action was to identify the constraint to improving the throughput of accounts payables. Hereafter, every type of transaction that was a "retouch" would be called a defect. So, for instance, unblocking a blocked invoice from a supplier wasn't just a natural piece of work in the accounts payables department, it was a defect. Had the upstream business process been executed with excellence, the invoice would never have been blocked. Based on that premise, the organization started to measure process defects. That number was sobering—6 million defects per year! It now had a target to aim at. However, the harder paradigm shift was yet to come.

Yazdi sensed that a large portion of the work done in the back-office shared services or GBS organization had to do with addressing defects created upstream. Hence GBS should focus on *reducing* these defects rather than just being efficient at *managing* them. Those defects needed to be removed even if they were occurring in another organization. The fact was that most of these 6 million defects were not being caused by Yazdi's Business Services organizations. They were due to business practices in other organizations, many of which *were operating as designed!* Specifically, half the blocked-invoice defects came from two buying departments—adult beverages and music CDs. In some cases, these two departments issued goods receipt notices in ways that resulted in quantity mismatches and thus invoices later getting blocked.

This was a process design issue in those departments. In theory, this wasn't Yazdi's problem. He could have communicated his findings to peers in the other departments and walked away. But at the same time, this framed the opportunity of *Unified Accountability* very well, and he firmly believed in that concept.

In hindsight, Yazdi did face a choice. He could accept his given responsibility for processing accounts payables transactions as is. Or he could assume accountability for the entire outcome of the quality of accounts payables, *even though many of the steps in the process were outside his organization.* To be clear, we're not talking about moving all people and budgets under one roof for this to occur. We're distinguishing between end-to-end *accountability* for the outcome on the one hand, and the distributed *responsibility* to execute different chunks of process on the other. And the latter can reside in other organizations.

What Challenges Had to Be Overcome?

Yazdi's next step upon assuming *Unified Accountability* was to convince other organizations to change their own business processes in the interest of improving the broader company's results as well as their own. This might sound like a no-brainer, but it is not. The issue is often related to conflicting goals. It's possible that the desired change is simply not convenient for the other organizations.

The key to addressing this issue is to talk with each senior stakeholder one on one. Perhaps the conversation with each business unit leader goes along the following lines—"This change will face resistance from some of your people. However, here's my commitment to you. I will deliver an x percent reduction in fraud cases, a y percent cost reduction, and a guaranteed twenty-four-hour service level commitment to your vendors. Can I enlist your support to this effort, driving the changes needed in the processes you control?"

It takes persistent pursuit of *Unified Accountability* to achieve defect elimination. It doesn't matter if the defects originate outside your organization. You must create a popular *movement* toward defect elimination via *Unified Accountability* through your ability to attract followers in other organizations, as Yazdi did. By exerting the power of *Unified Accountability*, he was able to eliminate 2 million blocked invoices or defects within nine months, thus helping the business with related people and cash advantages. Let's now move to our third driver, *Dynamic Operating Engine*, and yet another success story.

Driver #3. *Dynamic Operating Engine*: A Newly Created Fortune 100 Company Sets Up a *Dynamic Operating Engine* for Ongoing Business Process Superiority

Caroline Basyn, Strategy and Transformation lead for PepsiCo in Europe, is the person boards call when they have big organization transformation challenges. In a career spanning close to four decades, Caroline has played this role in a multitude of Fortune 100 companies. That's in addition to being mentor and coach for women executives through her leadership in the LEAD Network in Europe. Caroline's success story describes how she created a world-class Global Business Services organization at Mondelēz International. This operating model was created from scratch and was acknowledged as world-class within a handful of years.

Mondelēz International (Mondelez) had been created from Kraft Foods, the Fortune 100 multinational confectionary, food, and beverage conglomerate, in 2012. The prior year, Kraft Foods had announced plans to split into two publicly traded companies, an international snack-food company (Mondelēz) and a North American grocery company (Kraft Foods Group). Mondelēz had raced to a fast start, based on growth in the BRIC markets (Brazil, Russia, India, and China), only to find its business stalling as the four BRIC economies cooled off. With activist investor pressure on the board, the company swiftly pivoted to focusing on growing profit margins via a three-pronged strategy. One of those was to deliver a highly competitive business operation by forming a Global Business Services (GBS) organization. That's when Caroline's phone rang in 2014.

The Need for a Systemic Operating Model for Processes

When Caroline reported for work in October 2014, she had no strategy, no budget, and no people. In fact, her own cost was being borne by a transition budget. What she did have was a compelling mandate. She would need to create a new organization, GBS, that within three years would deliver cost savings and business process quality on par with or better than the competition. Since the work of the new GBS would come from different organizations, at different levels of maturity, and on different schedules, she needed an operating model—something that would routinely and consistently take in new work, transform it, and keep improving over time. She was expected not only to create one-time best-in-class GBS operations but also to create dynamic processes for long-term competitive advantage. In other words, she was expected to get to Stage 4 maturity of dynamic business processes.

The Foundation: Create a New GBS Organization

In typical fashion, Caroline strapped on her backpack and travelled to the Mondelēz locations around the world. This new GBS operating engine would not be built at the headquarters by consultants. It would be built *by* the Mondelēz people and *for* the Mondelēz people. It would incorporate the best-in-class experience previously acquired by Caroline at P&G.

Caroline's first step was to decide which business processes would be within the scope of GBS. That would be quickly followed by decisions about how the work would be sourced—that is, would it be done at the company's own offshore service centers, or would it be outsourced to vendors? The scope of work chosen to be moved first into GBS was record-to-report, order-to-cash, source-to-pay, and hire-to-retire. Within six months of starting, several key outsourcing contracts were signed, while in parallel, other work was moved to newly created offshore centers. Mondelēz outsourced the record-to-report processes to Genpact and the order-to-cash and source-to-pay processes to Accenture; it also set up three captive shared service centers in Costa Rica, Manila, and Bourneville for hire-to-retire.

Caroline's Approach: Build a *Dynamic Operating Engine* within GBS

The above GBS organization structure provided the foundation of re-sources. The actual dynamic operating model was the layer on top. The GBS operating model, managed via common playbooks and codified governance, would be identical across an ecosystem of insourced and outsourced delivery centers around the world. For every given functional service (e.g., HR), there would be two operating manuals or cookbooks—one for migrating the work into GBS and another for running operations. The cookbook for migration ensured that the transformation of the business process from the current Global Category model to the GBS model went through rigorous tollgates for streamlining processes and transitioning them to the new global model. The operations cookbook ensured that every business process acquired by GBS had clear, best-in-class methods for performance management, governance, and controls.

This disciplined approach paid off. Very quickly after the successful implementation of GBS and the dynamic operating model, more work was sent to GBS. That included consumer call centers, master data & analytical services, real estate & facility services, tax services, sales & marketing back office, and reporting services—all joining the same operating model.

What Challenges Had to Be Overcome?

Caroline's design for a dynamic business operations model would be based on five pillars. The cookbooks for migration and operations would lay out the activities across the following five pillars:

1. **Organization:** The first step was to design the right structure with the correct roles and skills for GBS. The new organization

had to have a mix of excellent business process knowledge, a business-centric mindset, and the ability to constantly reinvent itself, leveraging the newest AI/ML/NLP technology and digital capabilities.

2. **Governance:** This included two different management structures. One was the best-in-class procedures to manage vendors, such as Accenture and Genpact. The other was based on creating "customer team" partnerships with Mondelēz business unit leaders.

3. **Tools:** The migration and operations cookbooks were just the start. In addition, a whole new set of underlying systems and dashboards had to be created to run ever-improving business processes smoothly. For instance, there was a dashboard created for executive stakeholders for transparency and feedback on core performance metrics and priorities.

4. **Operations capabilities:** This was built on the principle of running business processes as if GBS were a business. In this context, "operations" included not just day-to-day transactional processes but also demand management of GBS services, financial pricing, innovation, quality assurance, risk management, controls, and so on.

5. **Financial discipline:** Each of the service managers in her GBS organization (e.g., Payroll Service manager, etc.) was treated like a general manager with end-to-end accountability for the specific service. This meant that financial performance metrics for the specific service had to be designed and delivered.

Caroline's plan was called GBS 2020. The basic design elements were very consistent with the steps to create a *Dynamic Operating Engine.* The model she built had clear methods and metrics for business-centric outcomes, a business engagement model, and a dynamic organization DNA for ongoing improvement.

Within three years, GBS had close to 5,000 employees, 12 global

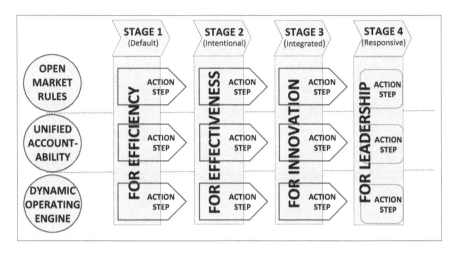

FIGURE 3: Action Steps for *Dynamic Process Transformation*

delivery centers, and 10 outsourced contracts. Caroline had exceeded her initial goals, having set up a GBS operation that would go on to accelerate the value created for the company over the next four years, by leveraging scale, standardization, and digitization, while eliminating waste and leakages and adding decision-making capabilities to provide visibility on increasing net revenue opportunities.

Creating a Practical Road Map— the Action Steps for *Dynamic Process Transformation*

The previous case studies from Francisco, Yazdi, and Caroline illustrate practical implementations of *Dynamic Process Transformation*. Each example highlighted only the one main driver involved. This was so that we could focus on each of the three drivers individually. Make no mistake, all three drivers were involved, even if the other two were less important in that specific context. That will be true for your own application of the *Dynamic Process Transformation* model. Depending on your situation, you will need a tailored mix of these three drivers, and that mix will change with time and maturity.

So, to get down to brass tacks—how does one implement the road map for *Dynamic Process Transformation?* To help you assemble the right plan for yourself, we offer twelve Lego-block-type action steps. You will need to build your own plan, based on your own organization's context, your starting point of process maturity, and your endpoint. Figure 3 depicts the concept of the Lego blocks or action steps. There are twelve because of the 4×3 matrix of four stages of maturity and three drivers. You should need only some of these unless you start from scratch and go for the ultimate dynamic process maturity.

These twelve action steps are discussed in depth in the following twelve chapters. Each of the twelve chapters includes one or more underlying models. We hope to help you create a tailored and practical road map, providing data and storytelling to bring the key insights to life.

PART II

Stage 1 of Business Processes—
Default Maturity

Stage 1: Default Maturity. Focuses on Efficiency

Action Steps for *Dynamic Process Transformation*

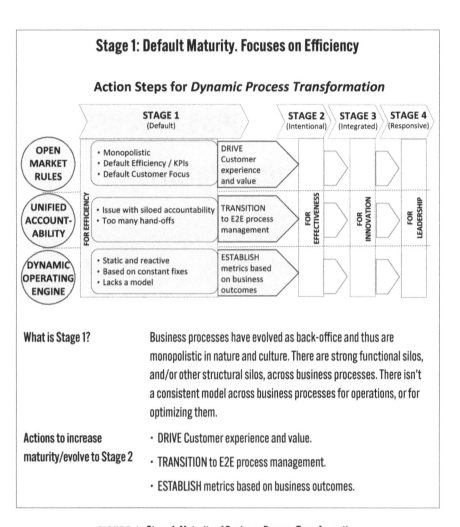

What is Stage 1?

Business processes have evolved as back-office and thus are monopolistic in nature and culture. There are strong functional silos, and/or other structural silos, across business processes. There isn't a consistent model across business processes for operations, or for optimizing them.

Actions to increase maturity/evolve to Stage 2

- DRIVE Customer experience and value.
- TRANSITION to E2E process management.
- ESTABLISH metrics based on business outcomes.

FIGURE 4: Stage 1, Maturity of Business Process Transformation

3

The Problem with Running Business Processes "as a Monopoly"

> **KEY INSIGHT:** Running business processes as if they were openmarket products is the key to avoiding process obsolescence.

Monopolistic business models have a harder time staying relevant and competitive over time. That's true for business processes too. Having said that, we must acknowledge that the original state of all business processes (i.e., Stage 1) is monopolistic both in structure and in mindset. Functions like IT, finance, and HR are initially created to operate and standardize processes. They are rewarded for being the enforcers of standards and for their ability to say no to things that are different. Standardization is a vital lever for streamlining processes and reducing costs.

So, how do we reconcile this with our driver of *Open Market Rules?* As with most things in life, there exist different degrees of *Open Market Rules.* Also, even at very loose *Open Market Rules,* there are benefits to being at this initial step (Stage 1). We don't want to miss that, but we don't want to stay there too long either. This chapter focuses on identifying the metaphorical baby in the bathwater at Stage 1 *Open Market Rules.* It also suggests how we should keep evolving to the next

stage. We will illustrate the features and challenges of this monopolistic business model with a personal anecdote—the Poste Italiane
transformation.

In 2015, Filippo was asked to serve on the board of Poste Italiane.
It was a critical time for the Italian postal service, for it planned to sell
40% of its shares on the stock market within a few months.[12] This
would be the country's largest state sell-off in 25 years and one of Europe's biggest IPO listings of the season. Being of Italian origin, Filippo
was honored to accept the request to serve. However, before we proceed further with developing the example of the privatization of Poste
Italiane, there is an important caveat. The use of a public sector example is not to suggest that public sector enterprises as a whole are less
efficient or effective than private companies. One has only to look at
some of the superefficient Singaporean state services to recognize that.
Or for that matter, the history of postal services through the ages. The
lessons we are mining for are related to the conditions necessary for
successful business process transformation.

How Poste Italiane Moved toward an Open Market Model

At the time, Poste Italiane was a 153-year-old national icon. Its annual
revenues were €28.5Bn, and it had businesses in logistics, savings, and
insurance. As with other national postal privatizations, this move was
not totally uncontentious. However, to understand why it was necessary, it is important to backtrack into the organization's past.

Implementing Poste Italiane's Privatization

By the early 1990s, the Italian postal service was already considered
unviable in terms of both efficiency and profitability. Its budget deficits
were driven by people costs, which in 1986 ate up about 93% of its revenue. Service outages and reputation issues were inevitable. However,
the need to privatize the post was eventually driven by macroeconomic
considerations. In 2014, Italy had the second-largest debt in the EU,
after Greece. The Italian prime minister pushed to sell off public assets

The Italian Postal Service's Historical Evolution

While the credit for developing the most advanced postal system in the ancient world goes to the Roman Empire, formal postal services existed for centuries before that. The Persian Empire had post-houses in the 6th century BCE; Egypt had postal services in 2000 BCE and China in 1000 BCE at the latest. Ancient postal services were critical information technology infrastructure to govern and secure far-flung regions of large empires.

The Roman Empire took this to the next level of efficiency and effectiveness. In 20 BCE the emperor Augustus created the amazing *cursus publicus*, the courier service of the Roman Empire, to transport messages, officials, and tax revenues from one province to another. However, with the fall of the Roman Empire, government-sponsored postal services all but disappeared.

Postal services reappeared in the Middle Ages, but this time they were owned by private businesses. Their founding was driven by the rise of global commerce and, with it, the need for international correspondence. Companies based in Italy, Russia, and France developed common infrastructure to carry orders and commissions and to effect settlements.

However, by the late 15th century, the balance of private versus government ownership of the postal service industry tilted back toward governments. This was caused by the rise of strong nation-states with centralized governments, such as in France and Britain. In the 18th, 19th, and early 20th centuries, postal services came to be the beloved services and technological phenomena that people still remember. Postal services drove the need for communication infrastructure, ranging from horse carriages to trains, airplanes, telephones, telegraph, print media, and many others. These were the glory days of postal services. What could possibly go wrong? Well, efficiency was a perennial issue. Three decades ago, it was jokingly said that Italy had two types of mail service—bad and worse. Over time, calls to restructure the Italian postal service only grew louder, and Poste Italiane made significant progress.

like the post to raise cash and to convince foreign investors that Italy was on the road to economic recovery.[13]

The trigger for transforming Poste Italiane may have been the country's debt situation, but to be clear, the business model for the post had all but crumbled. Letter post usage had declined. Digital communication technologies like fax and email, and the rise of the internet, were all eating into the volumes of postal mail. Around the world, postal services with their deep networks of post office branches started to move toward the more lucrative industries of banking, mobile telephony, and insurance. In Italy, that trend would be accelerated via the Poste Italiane transformation. Today, the new business model and the resulting processes currently support four major areas—mail and parcel, financial services, payments and mobile, and insurance services. The transformation has succeeded. Poste Italiane's share price rose by 71% in the six years following the date of listing, even while the FTSE MIB (the stock index of major companies listed on the Borsa Italiana) *decreased* by 20.8%. This delivered an overall return for shareholders (TSR) of 137% while the main Italian stock exchange index recorded a loss of 47%.

Learning from Poste Italiane about *Open Market Rules*

The transformation of Poste Italiane spins out multiple lessons for *Open Market Rules*. We examine several of the most critical ones here.

1. An open market demands ever-changing key performance indicators (KPIs).

Let's examine the operational situation at Poste Italiane in the early 2000s. There were established business processes as well as standard operations procedures (e.g., for running post office facilities, security services, repair, maintenance, etc.). KPIs existed as well (for timeliness of delivery, operating cost, security of the post, etc.). There existed the equivalent of "process owners"—that is, the administrators who establish standards. However, these people were not empowered to adjust these KPIs as the world changed, nor were they held accountable for the results. For instance, even as post office branches became less important in the world of fax, email, and the internet (driven by external open market forces), the reward systems for the "process owners" of post office branches were still based on old KPIs (e.g., efficient customer and letter processing at physical branches). The learning here is that although the starting or "default" KPIs tend to be well-intentioned, they become outdated as the world changes.

What was missing at Poste Italiane was the stimulus to go beyond these default efficiency-based KPIs.

2. Monopolistic business models can struggle when either customers or their needs change.

Despite ever-decreasing budgets, Poste Italiane employees were doing a heroic job of understanding and meeting the service needs of their clients. There was only one problem—they were focused on an increasingly obsolete definition of "the customer." As the postal service evolved from the letter delivery industry toward the broader communications and logistics industries, the target customer should have shifted. It wasn't just the average letter-receiving citizen. It should have also included the digitally oriented customer and ecommerce businesses, among others.

The learning here is that monopolistic business models find it difficult to evolve from their historical focus on default customers. This challenge of staying too long with a focus on historic or default customers is common to business process organizations as well.

The Model: *Open Market Rules* at Stage 1

You can avoid being caught flat-footed with default efficiency KPIs and a default customer focus by embracing the *Open Market Rules* for Stage 1. There are two actionable items here.

1. Drive high-efficiency KPIs.

To be clear, most organizations will have some KPI measurement and efficiency improvement programs even at the default efficiency KPI level. In a stable world, where the environment does not alter significantly over time, this may be fine. However, the world today is constantly changing—that is a core premise of this book. Also, if a KPI is defined a dozen different ways by a dozen different owners, then it will take perhaps a dozen different conversations to change the KPI. That slows down change.

Furthermore—and at times this is the more challenging issue—if the process owner (sometimes referred to as the *global* process owner or GPO) is somewhat disconnected from daily operations, they may, without meaning to, become a barrier to transformation. That may sound harsh, so let's illustrate this point, using call center operations as an example. Let's assume a situation where there is one default efficiency KPI—the time taken to resolve problems. The issue arises when different call centers interpret this metric differently—something that happens often at early stages of maturity. Perhaps one call center is very diligent in ensuring that the problem is completely solved before closing the ticket, while the other one is more aggressive in closing the ticket, whether or not the user's problem is fully resolved as deemed by the customer. The second center will have better-looking results on the KPI, but they are clearly delivering worse service. This type of situation is not uncommon in low-maturity organizations. It arises because the GPO has neither the time nor the experience nor the leadership to truly internalize the KPI implications. That limits the outcomes of the operations.

The answer to these situations is to drive high-efficiency KPIs. That's done by driving higher-quality measurement, choosing more actionable metrics, and strengthening the GPOs' accountability for KPIs. We will elaborate on these below.

a. Establish a baseline of cost and performance for the individual business processes, then improve metrics quality.

In organizations with default efficiency KPIs, the definition of these metrics can be uneven. We saw that in the previous example of call center operations. We suggest starting by standardizing KPI definitions. It is possible to start incrementally, beginning with the most critical ones for the business. After that, establish a fully agreed-to baseline. Most KPI metrics lose credibility because the starting base is either unclear or illogical. We need to address that and instill more rigor in the quality of the metrics data.

b. Select a few actionable performance metrics, based on business outcomes.

Ironically, process owners hurt their ability to improve operational KPIs by overdoing measurement. Focusing on a few "outcome" metrics for the business, and then on some selective in-process KPIs that directly impact these outcomes, is much better than creating a hodgepodge of internal operations performance items. For processes that span multiple areas and functions, it's important that the metrics be end-to-end. An example of this is the "perfect order" metric in a supply chain. It denotes the right product, delivered to the right place, at the right time, in the right condition. For customers, this aggregated metric is more meaningful than its individual components.

c. Strengthen accountability via a unified view of KPI performance results, with an owner assigned to orchestrate it.

We recommend an actionable cockpit of metrics, with drill-down capabilities, that's designed to provide issue-to-resolution actionability. That's because low-maturity KPI organizations have fragmented accountability for KPI results. That is despite having KPI process owners. They tend to play a higher-level governance role in the actual operations by setting standards and expectations. The issue is that often, by not being hands-on in the operations, they don't direct actions across organizations, where things need to change.

2. Drive high-efficiency customer focus.

Interestingly, the challenge in most monopolistic process organizations is that process owners legitimately feel that they *are* customer focused. In practice, though, there may be a couple of problems. The process owners may be reactive, and they may labor under an incomplete definition of "customer."

Let's take the first issue, that is, at Stage 1 the customer focus is reactive. It is driven by anecdotal needs or as issues arise. Furthermore, there are no processes to create a robust upward spiral of ever-improving service to users and stakeholders. This has less to do with intent than with rigor and completeness.

The second problem is that employees who execute business processes may not fully comprehend who the "customer" actually is. Here, we must distinguish between users and stakeholders. These are two different entities, but they are both *customers* in their own right. In a post office situation, the citizen seeking postal service is a user, whereas the shareholders and the leaders of the post office are would-be stakeholders. Furthermore, it is possible that the needs of users and stakeholders are different. For instance, the user of a post office might love to get white glove concierge service when trying to post a letter, but the stakeholders would frown at the cost of that extravagance.

The challenge with reactive, default customer focus is that we could miss important signals of the need for business transformation. This is true whether the signals come from users *or* stakeholders. The issue for users is simple to understand: even as business operations become more and more efficient, users' experiences may in fact get worse because their needs have changed.

On the stakeholders' side, default customer focus is arguably more challenging to manage. Stakeholders within an organization (executive managers, internal senior clients, Wall Street shareholders, government leaders, etc.) desire better experiences for users, but at ever-decreasing costs. It's possible that they could be making decisions to reduce service costs without recognizing the impact on their users.

Overall, the problem with default customer focus is that the employees actually operating the business process become the meat in the sandwich between the diverging needs of users and stakeholders.

The solution to this is to establish a disciplined mechanism for bringing to the table the needs of stakeholders, users, and process owners, and to balance them. A steering board can be formed to provide direction and resolve issues. As the customer focus grows sharper, in higher stages of maturity, there will be better approaches such as product/service management for managing business processes. We will go into more detail on this in later chapters, but at this stage creating a board will suffice.

In Closing

Put together, these action steps to drive high-efficiency KPIs and high-efficiency customer focus address the inertia that exists in Stage 1 operations. They create a foundation for the organizations to be exposed to changing KPIs and customer definitions. In the next two chapters, we cover how additional action steps related to the other two drivers—*Unified Accountability* and *Dynamic Operating Engine*—can help Stage 1 operations even further.

Checklist Items for Stage 1, *Open Market Rules*

To further strengthen your *Open Market Rules*, compare performance with the following Stage 1 characteristics:

- ☑ Performance metrics are siloed and static. They serve individual process clusters or functions, and they don't change enough with the changing business environment.

- ☑ KPIs are devised to drive continuous improvement—mostly in relation to operations efficiency and lower costs—and are primarily functionally focused.

☑ Performance reporting is often seen as not reflecting the reality of the operations, or not embraced by all stakeholders.

☑ Customer feedback from users and stakeholders is mostly used to improve process operations and is focused on costs rather than value creation; there isn't a systemic engagement model in place.

☑ Process owners see their role as defining standards rather than owning the business outcomes and supporting changes to stay abreast of the external business environment.

4

Going beyond Functional Silos

KEY INSIGHT: End-to-end process design is better than siloed process design. But unified accountability for process outcomes is even better.

The aviation industry is often held up as an example of process excellence. And while it is true that we all have our favorite horror stories of bags lost or flights cancelled, we must admit that those are statistically insignificant given the incredibly vast, complex scale of global aviation. If you think that the business processes in your own company are complex, try running an operation that moves 5 billion passengers every year, in roughly 25,000 commercial aircraft, via 15,000 airports located in 195 countries. And do that with over 99.999999% reliability. And just to make things interesting, do it in a decentralized organizational construct where laws, standards, and procedures are not as tightly controllable as within a single company. There is no single CEO-like entity and no hierarchy for single accountability. Yet this is the industry that provides the benchmark for operational reliability.

True, we can point to the fact that airplanes are massively engineered for reliability, but let's look beyond the machinery. The industry directly employs more than 11 million people with varying capabilities around the world. They operate everything from ticketing to airport operations, to aircraft maintenance, to luggage and food services. The fact that such a complex, decentralized, sprawling operation delivers reliable (albeit not always likable) results is a minor miracle.

There's much that the airline industry can teach us about business process excellence given its decentralized and complex setup. How has it minimized the defects that occur in handoffs from one team to another? And how does it address the organization issues of functional silos across thousands of companies? To help us learn, it might be useful to look at an example of a failure. A postmortem of a problem, however painful, can often be useful.

The Story of What Happened to Malaysia Airlines MH370

When I (Tony) first heard that Malaysia Airlines flight MH370 was missing on March 8, 2014, my heart sank. Airline disasters are thankfully rare. However, I had a personal connection with this news. I had recently returned to Cincinnati after a two-year stint in Asia and have friends on that continent. Thankfully, none of my contacts were directly affected. On the other hand, the chaos that unfolded over the next few days was horrific. Coverage from CNN and other 24x7 news channels went from shock, to hope, to despair, and then gave way to a confounding mystery. I am an aviation buff, so I have never stopped wondering what happened in the few hours after MH370 disappeared from radar. More so because it involved an uncommon lapse in a proven aviation process—that is, the handoff between air traffic controllers (ATCs).

A Cascade of Process Failures

MH370 took off from Kuala Lumpur for Beijing at 12:42 on March 8, 2014. Fariq Hamid, the first officer, was flying the airplane[14] while the pilot Zaharie Ahmad Shah handled the radios. Thirty-seven minutes into the journey, the flight approached the border of jurisdiction between the ATCs in Malaysia and Vietnam. At such borders, control is

What Really Happened to MH370?

Twelve hours after MH370 vanished, search-and-rescue teams from Malaysia, Singapore, and Vietnam began searching for debris in the South China Sea, northeast of Vietnam. Unfortunately, it was the wrong area for a search. After going off radar, MH370 had executed a set of evasive measures, eventually turning toward the South Pole. The many directional changes it made appeared to be indicative of an intent to escape detection.

One of the best reconstructions of what happened to MH370 comes from a superb journalistic piece in *The Atlantic*. According to the author, William Langewiesche, "a lot can now be known with certainty about the fate of MH370. First, the disappearance was an intentional act. It is inconceivable that the known flight path, accompanied by radio and electronic silence, was caused by any combination of system failure and human error. Bolstering the idea that this was an act by the pilot, forensic examinations of Zaharie's simulator by the FBI revealed that he experimented with a flight profile roughly matching that of MH370—a flight north around Indonesia followed by a long run to the south, ending in fuel exhaustion over the Indian Ocean."

To be clear, it is extremely unlikely that avoiding any of the ATC handoff or other process breakdowns would have saved the passengers. Stopping a crash would have been almost impossible. However, because several of the parties involved in the first hour didn't follow protocol, the probability of finding the wreckage and black boxes in time is near zero. That has denied grieving family members some measure of closure.

passed from one ATC to the next via a prescribed handoff process. In line with this, the controller at Kuala Lumpur Center radioed the pilot the coordinates of the Vietnamese ATC: "Malaysian three-seven-zero, contact Ho Chi Minh one-two-zero-decimal-nine. Good night." Zaharie responded with a laconic, "Good night. Malaysian three-seven-zero." Interestingly, the pilot did not read back the coordinates as required. This is pertinent and was likely related to Zaharie's frame of mind. It was the last word heard from MH370. The airplane disappeared from

ATC radar a few seconds later. It vanished precisely at the seam of responsibility between the two ATCs, during the handoff process. The next step in ATC handoff would have been for Zaharie to call Vietnam ATC, or, failing that, for the controller to follow up and raise the alarm. These procedures were not followed.

The disappearance of an airplane from ATC radar is extremely unusual. As it happened, the ATC at Kuala Lumpur was busy dealing with other traffic and did not notice it. When he did check later, he assumed that the airplane was out of his range and being safely managed by Ho Chi Minh ATC. Meanwhile, the Vietnamese ATC, who should have heard from the pilot, tried to contact the airplane, without success. They failed to follow a guideline that requires them to inform the sending ATC if a pilot does not check in within five minutes of being handed off. By the time they contacted the controller at Kuala Lumpur, the plane had been off the radar for 18 minutes.

As is often the case in aviation disasters, it takes a perfect storm of many failures to create a catastrophe. In this situation too, many of the expected processes that should have kicked in, failed. Malaysian Aeronautical Rescue Coordination Centre should have been notified within an hour of the disappearance. It was not. It would be four hours before they were notified. Meanwhile, the plane continued to fly within the range of multiple radar systems belonging to four different countries[15] and the Malaysian military. Yet little was done with the data in the immediate hours after the plane disappeared. Unfortunately, after that it was just too late to help the aircraft.

Learning about Process Reliability from the Aviation Industry

The MH370 crash is thankfully an outlier when it comes to operational process breakdown. It was most likely an outcome of rogue human action. As mentioned earlier, aviation industry operational processes are characterized by high reliability *despite* decentralized, complex, and fragmented execution. How has the industry achieved that?

To understand how aviation has achieved process excellence, we need to back up a bit. It's helpful to first understand the various stages involved in improving business processes. In general, business processes achieve excellence via five discrete layers of action:

1. **Fix non-standard processes:** This is the starting point. Imagine what might happen if there were different steps for each country, or each airline, when it came to handling ATC control transfers. That's the first step in improving processes.

2. **Synchronize siloed processes:** Imagine if ATCs were standard but siloed off from other aviation processes, such as airport gate management. Handoff errors would result. This step addresses that.

3. **Execute E2E processes consistently:** Assume that terminal check-in to gate management to ATC processes have been synchronized but executional discipline is spotty. That can occur because it takes time to stabilize processes. Handoff errors may still occur.

4. **Add robust fail-safe designs to E2E process execution:** Assume that processes from terminal check-in all the way to ATC are well executed. However, if no fail-safe procedures have been designed for the rare situations where problems occur, there will be occasional blowups. That's because of the fact that while processes are efficient E2E, there is no *Unified Accountability* for an employee to circumvent or fix perfect-storm-type issues.

5. **Design roles for *Unified Accountability* of outcomes:** At this stage employees are empowered both to achieve near-zero defects and to constantly evolve processes to keep up process excellence.

Applying these layers to our work on business process maturity, we can see that all five items could cause process gaps at Stage 1 business process maturity. Most often, organizations have plans to get to the first three. Standardization, E2E process management, and following disciplines to improve execution are common. It is the final two—further reducing handoffs and designing roles for *Unified Accountability* of outcomes—that are less developed. We will use the aviation story to mine for lessons on these two.

1. Airline operations have perfected handoffs and built fail-safes.

Let's revisit the ATC handoff error between Malaysia and Vietnam. Its failure is shocking, given that several layers of process excellence were present. There are strict protocols governing the handoff of control of the airplane between the two controllers. Furthermore, there is always a single and clear accountability for control for each step in the process. There is also formal recognition of when accountability passes from one person to the next. Finally, such handoffs have fail-safe backups built in where needed. This is true of most operational processes in aviation, from takeoff procedures to gate management.

By contrast, business processes in most organizations still struggle with siloed accountability. Take for instance the order-to-cash (O2C) or the expanded quote-to-cash (QTC) business process, which runs from taking customer orders, to processing them in an IT system, to delivering the product via logistics operations, to collecting the cash from customers. There is on average a 30% loss of efficiency in operating this across the siloed functions of sales, IT, logistics, and finance. And that loss doesn't account for the impact on sales growth. A study by McKinsey[16]—one that is specific to the business-to-business (B2B) area—suggests that businesses that optimize QTC for end-to-end accountability significantly outperform peers that do not. They grow four times versus competition by adding more new accounts, expanding existing accounts, and retaining them at higher rates. And the opportunity only grows when country and regional organization silos are factored in. By the way, global process owners cannot help much with handoff issues at early stages of maturity. They are not involved in the actual execution of transactions.

2. The aviation industry has depth of *Unified Accountability* for E2E outcomes.

The aviation industry consists of a multitude of independent organizations that must come together if each passenger's journey is to be successful—airport terminals, airlines, baggage handling, ATC, security, maintenance, the aircraft crew, and so on. Yet when it comes to the most important E2E outcomes (i.e., keeping to travel schedules and passenger security), there is always single-point accountability at each step. During boarding, the gate agent has *Unified Accountability*, in the air the ATC has it, and so on. Having a single person accountable for E2E outcomes at key steps in the process is a core feature of aviation's design for process reliability.

One could argue that most business organizations do have *Unified Accountability* for business processes at the senior leadership level. After all, most functional leaders (sales, finance, and so on) report to the CEO, or in some cases to a COO. That design should allow end-to-end collaboration for business processes, shouldn't it? The challenge with that design is that it preserves functional silos (e.g., sales, IT, supply chain) as the primary reward structure, and does so all the way down the organization. So we end up relying on everyone's sense of "corporate citizenship" to optimize the end-to-end process, *even if that means suboptimizing their own functional one.* That's hard.

The design for *Unified Accountability* for E2E outcomes needs to cascade deep down within each business process. Let's dig deeper into how this might be achieved. In our hypothetical O2C example, would this mean having one employee run the entire O2C activity for a given order, from negotiation to collection? Absolutely not! We know that's simply unviable for most organizations. It is possible to have both *specialization of tasks* (i.e., an ATC's job is pretty narrow) and *Unified Accountability* (i.e., an accountability and reward system that puts end-to-end outcomes ahead of efficient functional task completion). Airline operations have perfected the art of not just designing end-to-end operations but also driving *Unified Accountability* for customer outcomes deep into each and every person in the operations.

Both learnings from the aviation industry (i.e., stronger process handoffs and deeper *Unified Accountability*) are built into our model for Stage 1 *Unified Accountability*.

The Model: *Unified Accountability* at Stage 1 Maturity

At Stage 1 maturity, accountability for E2E outcomes doesn't really exist. Even at senior levels in the organization, while there may be strong accountability to deliver outcomes within their own functions, it is unlikely that accountability for the end-to-end business process exists broadly. To address this, the lessons from the earlier analysis of the aviation industry regarding handoffs and deeper *Unified Accountability* can be reapplied. The model for *Unified Accountability* at Stage 1 has the following two parts.

1. Reduce handoff errors by standardization and E2E automation.

To be clear, even at Stage 1 maturity levels, most organizations do have programs for process standardization and automation. The issue isn't with the intent, but with the approach. Different business units, or functions, or countries, may believe they are each in the best position to define their own standards. For example, they may insist that their choice of IT systems is best for their needs. Sometimes, in a nod to promoting E2E process coordination, these organizations appoint global process owners (GPOs). GPOs normally provide standards and direction for processes (payroll, accounting, order management, etc.) They also work across process silos to improve E2E process efficiency. Additionally, the GPOs may have a community of practice (COP) to share knowledge and implement standards across the entire company. So, what is missing?

At issue is the effectiveness of these early structures. The control of process and automation standards still lies firmly in siloed functions, countries, or business units. The GPO and COP structures are not empowered to make decisions. We need to accelerate their journey of maturity through Stage 1. Here's how to do that.

a. If E2E GPO roles or COPs don't exist, then create them. If they exist, then accelerate their maturity by changing their success metrics. Those need to shift from recommending practices to delivering business outcome goals (e.g., the cost of the process and/or the length of the cycle time for all business units must be reduced by 10% around the world).

b. Capture, analyze, and improve the data related to process-handoff losses. Handoff losses are productivity killers. Each retouch must be viewed as a loss. We have experienced this in our personal lives. If your doctor, who has all your medical records, has referred you to a specialist and that person's office has you fill out your detailed medical history all over again, then you've felt this. This is true for business processes too. At this stage, we must measure and improve all such handoff losses.

c. Change the success metrics for standardization of IT systems. The successful implementation of IT systems is merely an in-process goal. The true outcome must be seamless and touchless operation of business processes—end-to-end. Siloed IT systems for parts of the organization, or for parts of the business process, don't fully address the complete issue of corporate productivity.

d. Where possible, leapfrog IT systems and data architectures. Today's modern technology and IT architectures don't need technology standardization to be completed before we can build further process excellence. For instance, a few decades ago, P&G standardized its core IT platform, called Enterprise Resource Planning (ERP), to use SAP software. This single platform could run all core business processes (finance, HR, manufacturing, logistics, sales, and distribution) across all businesses and all countries. This was a remarkable achievement, which is unattainable today even for many mature companies. However, the truth is that if we were to target the same business process outcomes today, we could do it with more advanced technology that could deliver the same results despite having multiple ERPs. We would not need to get it down to one ERP. Organizations that are at early stages of process and systems maturity can certainly leapfrog today.

2. Drive E2E *Unified Accountability* deeper into the organization.

Our second action item is to drive *Unified Accountability* deeper in the organization. When this is not done, it disempowers employees from doing the right thing from a broader company perspective. The recommended action step in our model is to start evolving the organization structure and the reward systems. This incentivizes E2E outcomes among the process employees. In our earlier O2C process example, it would be much more motivating for the individuals entering sales orders into the system to be thinking of themselves as helping meet targets such as *deliver sales revenue, days sales outstanding* (DSO), and *accurate customer service*, as opposed to viewing their role as data entry operators for orders. The fact that they are at a junior level in the organization shouldn't prevent us from empowering them so as to hold them accountable for both efficiency and effectiveness in their scope of work.

When promoting individual E2E *Unified Accountability*, desiloed operations organizations like GBS (Global Business Services) are best. They can be much more effective than the siloed, functional structures of the past. For historical context, organization structures in the early twentieth century were task specialized (e.g., Henry Ford's specialization of labor). That went best with a hierarchical or functional organization structure. By the 1980s it was evident that businesses now needed flexibility and speed in addition to efficiency if they were to thrive. Thus was born the matrix structure, whereby employees or units could have more than one line of reporting managers. Although organization structures evolved from *Hierarchical/Functional* to *Matrixed*, information and data to run internal business processes remained largely unchanged. Some matrixed reporting lines were introduced, for functional employees, but by and large the internal information and process flow stayed static. That issue has presented a significant opportunity with the rise of the information revolution and digitally native competition. That is where enabling E2E *Unified Accountability* via GBS type structures can be a powerful lever for change.

So, how should we accelerate the evolution of *Unified Accountability*–based organization structures (like a GBS)? Here are the initial steps to get going:

a. Charter a study to determine the functional processes that could be aggregated into a centralized "shared services" organization. Assign a multifunctional team, sponsored by senior leaders, to conduct the study and formulate a recommendation.

b. Define the scope of the work by applying the following best-in-class principles: processes that are common across business units/markets, that are transactional in nature, and that can be "operationalized" are candidates for this newly created organization.

c. Assign a leader to this organization and establish a leadership team to support that person. Such a team can be pragmatically formed, initially, by the process owners of the work in scope (HR, finance, IT, etc.). This team's deliverable is an integrated business plan, which must include minimum price and service-level commitments as well as strategies for greater value creation.

d. Migrate the process operations from the functional organizations to centralized "shared services." We recommend doing this in stages, as opposed to a "big bang," following the proven model of transferring the people (reporting line), their costs (budget), and their work all at the same time.

e. Redesign rewards and recognition programs for employees to strengthen delivery of E2E process outcomes.

In Closing

While organization designs have evolved over the centuries into more sophisticated and matrixed structures, until recently the information availability (across the company and beyond) prevented business processes from following suit. Consequently, decision-making within business processes, whether O2C, supply chain planning, or even new hire onboarding, remained functionally siloed. With the rise of digital technology, the opportunity to make business processes not just more efficient but also dynamic has bloomed. The challenge presented by functionally siloed accountability relates to much more than the 30% loss of efficiency noted earlier by the McKinsey study. Such siloing misses out on the unlimited positive opportunity of *Unified Account-ability*. The good news is that these opportunities can be addressed and even codified via newer operating models. In the next chapter we will expand on how to accomplish this.

Checklist Items for Stage 1, *Unified Accountability*

To strengthen *Unified Accountability*, compare performance with the following Stage 1 characteristics:

- ☑ Process ownership is limited within the functional scope and priorities; there is a lack of harmonization and consistency across different processes.

- ☑ Processes are not managed end-to-end; to the extent a process extends through multiple areas or functions, different people are responsible for each single part. Significant handoff issues and losses occur.

- ☑ Focus is mostly on siloed process efficiency rather than on E2E outcomes deep within the organization. As a result, key customer outcomes are suboptimized.

- ☑ The reward system of process operations is based mainly on siloed or functional cost reductions and reliability, as opposed to E2E company or E2E customer. GBS-like structures that promote E2E process outcomes don't exist.

- ☑ The IT systems for standardization and automation are siloed as well. They are not yet ready to eliminate system touches between siloed processes or functions.

5

Don't Undermine Good Strategy with Poor Operating Models

> **KEY INSIGHT:** Operating models turn strategy into action at a company level. This applies to business processes too. Having a deliberate *Dynamic Operating Engine* is critical for sustained process excellence.

Setting the right goals for business process efficiency, effectiveness, and innovation is only half the battle. The other half is to have a reliable model to turn these goals into day-to-day actions throughout the organization. That's where an operating model (operating engine) comes in.

These process operating engines need to be (a) consistent and (b) dynamic in their ability to evolve with the market. Regarding consistency in operating models, the way a company does finance, or HR, may vary depending on the business units or countries or subsidiaries. Acquisitions and divestitures introduce even more variations. Consequently, the way business processes handle their operations, continuous improvement, measurement, and so on vary significantly. Thus, at early Stage 1 maturity, there is no deliberate or consistent operating model to turn process goals into daily operations.

When it comes to the need for dynamic processes, in the "real" business world, most business processes within companies evolve organically and slowly. That creates a widening gap between the dynamic market need and the reality of slow-paced process change. That's where a *Dynamic Operating Engine* comes in. We need to establish this consistency and dynamism within Stage 1 maturity. For doing that, we can learn from stories from other industries on how to create the best operating models. In this case, we examine one of the most successful large business turnarounds in history—Ford Motors in 2006.

How Alan Mulally Engineered Ford's Turnaround

Alan Mulally's Ford Motors turnaround in 2006 has been referred to as the biggest turnaround in business history.[17] We might debate the precision of that claim, but it is unquestionably among the best examples of an operating model transformation. At the time Mulally arrived from Boeing in 2006, the automaker had just posted a record loss for the year of $12.7Bn. By 2010, Ford had posted a net income of $6.6Bn, and Ford's stock had appreciated more than 1,000% from its 2008 recession lows. That's a remarkable change by most standards, and what makes it even more exceptional is how it was done. Turnaround strategies range from slash-and-burn approaches to shed costs, to sublime transformations in organizational culture. Mulally's approach was based on the latter. It provides our topic of *Dynamic Process Transformation* with key lessons on the importance of a strong operating model. Whenever there is a persistent gap between strategy and execution, the culprit is usually the operating model,[18] which refers to *how* the business model is brought to life to deliver customer value. Successful transformation of an operating model, especially in established companies, is really, really hard to accomplish. Thus, this story gives us a great set of lessons to apply to Stage 1 *Dynamic Operating Engines*.

When Alan Mulally started at Ford, he quickly realized that the employees were very busy and stretched to their limits. But the balance between time spent on internal meetings and time spent on external customer value was off.[19] We usually encounter this situation when an operating model is not functioning: people are very busy working on *urgent* tasks and don't have time for the *important* ones. Also, Ford's operations were having a tough time associating employees with individual accountability for business results. The measurement system for business performance was broken. Most leaders felt that their results on the scorecards were "green" (i.e., on track), yet the business as a whole was wildly off target. This too is typically a strong indication of a poor operating model.

Changing the Operating Model and Culture at Ford

Mulally decided to reapply the model of Business Plan Review (BPR) meetings, which he had used while he was at Boeing. BPRs involved weekly meetings in which every department had to break down its efforts and report them in ways that indicated measurable progress. They became core to his strategy for eliminating nonproductive meetings while driving more accountability among employees for their own results.

There is a telling anecdote about how the BPR process was initially received by Ford's leaders. At his first BPR meeting, Alan Mulally asked the company's 16 top leaders if they were in the green, yellow, or red on their top five priorities. Almost everyone responded that their priorities were green. Yet Ford was projected to lose $17Bn that year. Obviously, it was unlikely that all priorities were on track. Mulally asked, "So, is our business plan to lose $17 billion this year? If the answer to that question is yes, then we are in the green. Otherwise, we are not!" Eventually, one leader admitted to being in the red. Mulally applauded him and thanked him for his honesty rather than criticizing him for being in the red. Mulally would go on to implement a new, transparent operations culture.

From an organization design perspective, Mulally moved Ford from a structure of regional business units into a global functional model. This enabled the company to drive more efficient and effective operations, for example, by reducing the number of vehicle platforms. Mulally called his approach "One Ford."[20] The idea was almost deceptive in its simplicity: to run Ford as one company, with one set of products. He wanted to cut the 97 models by more than two-thirds. That helped the company focus on improving the quality, desirability, and profitability of the cars and trucks sold under its core brand. At the same time, Mulally restructured costs, reducing pension and medical liabilities as well as the number of plants and employees.

Thanks to the new strategy and the operating model redesign (i.e., moving to a global functional structure, increasing individual accountability, and rationalizing the number of vehicle platforms), Ford returned to profitability over the next four years. It even survived the 2008 economic crisis without a bailout from the American taxpayer.

The Broader Picture:
Ford's Problems Were Part of the Bigger US Auto Industry Pattern

There's an important epilogue to our Mulally story, though. We must put Ford's problems in the context of the broader US auto industry picture—specifically, the erosion of the US auto industry's once dominant market share over the preceding half-century. The reality is that the decline of the once-powerful big auto companies is part of a pattern. Much of the literature on the issues facing US automakers has pointed to their business model (their focus on creating big and powerful cars, union labor costs, productivity issues, unanticipated spikes in oil prices, etc.). That literature is accurate as far as it goes, but it is also incomplete, for it does not hold the industry's leaders accountable for their shortcomings in terms of operating models.

The fact is that early warning signs for US automakers were present as early as the 1950s. They failed to heed closely the emergence of Volkswagen in the United States and the appeal of smaller cars. Profit trumped design and quality, whereas in Japan, the corporate culture emphasized both. That would later pay huge dividends for Japanese companies. The 1970s oil crisis then suddenly exposed the problem of overreliance on an outdated business and operating model. For instance, the operating model focused on mass production techniques, with large volumes of vehicles manufactured against a fixed and rigorous schedule for raw materials, labor, and sales. In fact, flexibility in operations was viewed as a threat to standardization. Fast forward

Clarifying the Difference between a Business Model and an Operating Model

In the previous section we used the term "operating model" frequently. While most people are familiar with the terms operating model and business model, it is worth clarifying the distinction between the two, because our driver of *Dynamic Operating Engine* is fundamentally a dynamic version of an operating model, as applied to business processes.

The simplest way to distinguish between a business model and an operating model is that the former describes *how a business captures value*, while the latter is *how a business is run*. Let's stay with the example of an automobile company. It designs, produces, and sells cars. That involves suppliers, customers, and the value added by the company. The resulting products are more valuable than the sum of all the raw material inputs. How the business captures value in the marketplace is driven by the business model.

Operating models *turn high-level corporate strategies into operational outcomes*. The operating model can be somewhat simplistically represented by the people, processes, and technologies that bring the business model to life on a day-by-day level. That is, it refers to how all the components of a business model work together. Fixing a broken operating model can be one of the smartest investments an executive can make. A study done by Bain Consulting of companies in 8 industries and 21 countries found that companies with top-quartile operating model indicators—those with clear, robust operating models—have five-year compound average revenue growth and operating margins respectively 120 and 260 basis points higher than those in the bottom quartile.

to today, and it becomes obvious that the 1970s-era operating model wasn't a one-time glitch for the US automakers. Even as car designs, manufacturing, labor, and other cost elements have become comparable between US and foreign automakers, the market share for US automakers has steadily declined. It's evident that they have been less flexible than the competition when it comes to evolving their operations. More importantly, we must note that this performance volatility is despite the fact that the big US auto players have transformed themselves several times each. All of this brings home the point that one-off operating model transformations are not necessarily sustainable. The operating model itself must be dynamic; it needs to evolve as business conditions change.

Learning from Ford about *Dynamic Operating Engines*

Ford's success story illustrates an important fact about the relationship between business models and operating models. An organization has a far better chance at succeeding when its operating model is aligned with its business model, fully supporting it. Business models tend to be the sexy sibling. They get an oversized share of attention. Operating models don't get as much attention because they represent executional rigor. There are two key lessons that can be applied to our *Dynamic Process Transformation* work at Stage 1: first, the operating model must be in sync with the business model, and second, the operating model must be dynamic so as to keep changing over time.

1. **Mulally designed an operating model that was in sync with his business model.**

As mentioned earlier, the operating model represents the day-to-day processes for executing the company's business model. If day-to-day operations scorecards are all green while the business results are all deep red, then clearly the two are out of sync. That's a very important lesson for Stage 1 business process transformation. In early stages of business process maturity, the internal functional processes don't always line up to deliver the end business outcome. What's missing is a methodology or an engine that forces synchronization. Mulally's BPR meetings were a minor but clear illustration of this type of methodology.

Mulally also simplified and scaled both the product platform and internal functional processes. Recall that the "One Ford" strategy was to run the organization as a single company; this entailed streamlining functional processes as well as slashing the number of vehicle platforms. Applying the one company concept to Stage 1 process maturity organizations is a huge idea. The fact is that in early stages of maturity, internal process disciplines are different for different business units or countries. We have not "one operating engine" but several. These can be reduced to a single operating engine and then scaled to deliver higher efficiency.

2. Ford and other US automakers have paid the price for not having a dynamic operating model.

The second key lesson is that operating models need to evolve. Once again, much of the current literature on business agility focuses on reinventing products and ignores the need for a dynamic operating model. The volatile performance of the US automakers over the decades serves as a critical reminder that for sustained competitive advantage, a dynamic operating model is a must.

Applying these lessons to Stage 1 can be very beneficial. As mentioned earlier, the reality for early Stage 1 organizations is that they have not just one operating engine, but many. As we streamline that, it's important to choose an operating engine that is known to be dynamic. By dynamic, we mean an operating engine that continuously adapts itself to changing customer needs, business priorities, and market conditions. This prevents the process operating model from falling out of sync with the business model over time. However, for the moment, our process maturity work will focus mainly on getting from many operating engines to one. In future stages we will keep strengthening its ability to stay dynamic. In the next paragraph, we outline such a model for a Stage 1 *Dynamic Operating Engine* and share how this can be achieved.

The Model: *Dynamic Operating Engine* for Stage 1

The model for creating a *Dynamic Operating Engine* at Stage 1 liberally reapplies the lessons from Ford's turnaround as well as from the broader US auto industry. Specifically, the operating model must be in sync with the business model. Also, we want to have one operating model, not many. And finally, the operating model must be dynamic. In our process operations work, we will share a model that is in sync with business needs and is able to evolve dynamically. We refer to it simply as an operating *engine* rather than an operating *model*, because it applies only to internal process work. (Operating models, by contrast, would apply to a company's product as well as to its internal process work). Our *Dynamic Operating Engine* has two action items.

1. Develop one operating engine that is in sync with business needs.

During legacy, early-stage maturity levels, business processes deliver siloed functional efficiencies (e.g., within finance, or sales, or HR). The company has many operating engines, and while the individual processes sync well within their siloed functions or business units, they don't scale well across the silos. We can get going on the Stage 1 *Dynamic Operating Engine* simply by asking three questions. The answers to these will provide the foundation for creating the "one" operating engine.

a. Are we managing our business processes end-to-end (E2E)?

Most businesses start out with siloed business processes. So, as mentioned in the previous chapter, we may have order-taking business processes, separate from order fulfillment, which in turn is separate from collecting cash. This is as opposed to viewing these activities as part of one E2E process called order-to-cash (O2C). There is a finite list of such end-to-end business processes that are needed to run a company. The most common ones are hire-to-retire, record-to-report, procure-to-pay, order-to-cash, and idea-to-offering. These will certainly be different for different industries, but it is easy enough to pick the top five in most companies. Figure 5 provides a list of end-to-end work processes that the SAP software supports.[21]

b. Do we know the cost of our business processes E2E?

The first question leads to an important follow-up—how are we to measure the efficiency of each E2E? The issue with a process that is siloed (as opposed to being E2E) and fragmented in accountability (as opposed to having an E2E process owner) is that it becomes difficult to design for E2E efficiency. An important start here is to ask questions

ATR	Acquire to Retire
FTD	Forecast to Delivery
HTR	Hire to Retire
ITO	Idea to Offering
ITR	Issue to Resolution
MTO	Market to Order
OTC	Order to Cash
PTI	Plan to Inventory
PTP	Plan to Produce
PTP	Procure to Pay
QTC	Quote to Cash
RTR	Record to Report

FIGURE 5: E2E Process List Examples

about the full E2E cost of the business process. Measuring the E2E cost of a business process, such as cost of OTC per order or RTR per business unit, provides more relevant benchmarks and helps generate systemic accountability end-to-end, which is one of the enablers for a dynamic operating model.

c. Do we know the number of touch points within each E2E process?

The previous question helps us understand the efficiency of the E2E processes; this one starts to indicate how well they are streamlined. It is important to avoid the trap of loosely wrapping up siloed and frag-mented processes and calling it an E2E process. The number of touch points (i.e., how many times a transaction is manually touched by a person) is a good proxy for how well the E2E process is integrated.

Asking these three questions will facilitate the design of a *Dynamic Operating Engine*, which is our second action step.

2. Design the operating engine to be scalable and flexible.

This step codifies the discipline of managing all business processes, but in a manner that can scale over time. Our intent is to create an operating engine that isn't specific to a single point in time. For in-stance, if the operating engine design is heavily reliant on offshoring the business process work to low-cost vendors because the priority at the time is cost reduction, it's possible that this design will become a bottleneck when rapid growth becomes the priority. It's important to design the operating engine to be scalable and flexible in order to keep it in sync with changing customer needs, business priorities, and market conditions. Building such a dynamic engine entails nine steps, which together cross all business processes in the company.

a. Define the scope of scalable business processes.

Specifically, define the criteria according to which the organization can decide which parts of the process should be centralized and scaled as well as which parts should reside within the business unit or function.

b. Design the methodology to transition work successfully.

Once step 1 is complete, we need an approach that enables us to move process work and people from the business unit or function to the centralized process group. Two-thirds of such transitions fail, which is why a methodology is crucial. This is where standard approaches and cookbooks, like the one from the Mondelēz story in Chapter 2, can help.

c. Define your operations management methodology.

Design the methodologies for running process operations of the highest quality. These are the methodologies for constantly improving process quality and cost. For example, they could be based on methodologies like six-sigma.

d. Create the model to best leverage vendors.

Define the method for purchasing standard services (e.g., payroll processing, or IT servers) externally, as opposed to building them in-house. Also, define the method for governing these optimally.

e. Institute practices of internal client management.

These are the methods for ensuring that business process managers can constantly and tightly stay in tune with business priorities.

f. Organize and run processes by applying product management practices.

Product management practices force the organization to be disciplined when it comes to being aware of customer needs, cost structures, external environmental changes, and the like. This is an excellent model to apply to business processes.

g. Institute professional performance management.

The art of choosing and communicating the right metrics for performance management of processes is core to ongoing improvements as well as to building trust in the business processes.

h. Define your financial model for business processes.

Institute the approach and steps to price and recover the cost of each business process. Following a professional model provides transparency regarding the costs and benefits of each business process.

i. Design your process organization structure.

This involves a deliberate choice of how to organize your people and models for agility, innovation, and business-centricity. A good organization model will also allow for a *Dynamic Operating Engine*.

In our experience, we have found extremely strong correlations between the best methods to run the company itself and the operating engines for running best-in-class process operations. The above model is based on business management principles and has enabled us to create, run, and advise on some of the most competitive operations in the world.

In Closing

The need to strengthen operating models has continued to gain traction at the board level. The previously cited Bain study suggests that most companies consider it to be a top-three priority. However only one-fifth of executives in that study felt that their operating model offered a competitive advantage. Organizations have a long way to go in implementing strong operating models.

Similarly in the case of internal business processes, the authors' combined experience of seven decades indicates that most companies are still at the Stage 1 maturity of *Dynamic Operating Engines*. Companies continue to focus on pursuing efficiency goals. To be fair, standardization and automation still have tremendous untapped value and hence currently rule operations-related strategies. However, in today's digital world, choosing between flexibility and efficiency is not an option. Process operating engines must be dynamic.

This chapter rounds out the Stage 1 maturity of the three drivers of business process transformation (i.e., *Open Market Rules, Unified Accountability,* and *Dynamic Operating Engine*). In general, Stage 1 maturity delivers on process efficiency, which translates into lower costs. But it's not adaptive and doesn't fully evolve as the needs of the business change. The next three chapters focus on Stage 2 or *intentional* business processes. Going from Stage 1 to 2 helps organizations focus on both operational efficiency and effectiveness.

Checklist Items for Stage 1, *Dynamic Operating Engine*

To strengthen the *Dynamic Operating Engine,* compare performance with the following Stage 1 characteristics:

- ☑ The process scope is driven by the organization structure rather than by the end-to-end process definition.

- ☑ The modus operandi involves delivering what each individual business unit or function needs, as opposed to developing a two-way synergistic interdependency.

- ☑ Processes have been automated and digitized to a large extent; however, the value to the organization's bottom line is not always clear.

☑ There is a gap between the process operations organization and the business, in the perceptions of performance and business value being delivered.

☑ There is no consistent operating model underlying how business processes are run across the enterprise. Even if one exists, it is static and doesn't keep up with changing times.

PART III

Stage 2 of Business Processes—
Intentional Maturity

Stage 2: Intentional Maturity. Focuses on Effectiveness

Action Steps for *Dynamic Process Transformation*

STAGE 1	STAGE 2	STAGE 3	STAGE 4
(Default)	(Intentional)	(Integrated)	(Responsive)

OPEN MARKET RULES
- Business value focus
- Outcome-based KPIs

FOCUS on process effectiveness

UNIFIED ACCOUNT-ABILITY
- End-to-end focus
- Strong processes but with some overlaps

RUN processes as products

DYNAMIC OPERATING ENGINE
- Transparency of E2E process costs
- Transparency of business value
- Performance tracking

PROFESSIONALIZE business engagement

FOR EFFICIENCY · FOR EFFECTIVENESS · FOR INNOVATION · FOR LEADERSHIP

What is Stage 2?

Business processes are built and operated E2E, aimed at generating effectiveness for the customer, in addition to efficiency. Performance metrics (KPIs) are sufficiently outcome-based, including customer experience, built around transparency and business value creation.

However, business operations are still run as back-office. Any transformation requires an ad hoc intervention, there are process overlaps in places, and innovation is erratic and inconsistent.

Actions to increase maturity/evolve to Stage 3

- FOCUS on strengthening process effectiveness.
- RUN processes as product.
- PROFESSIONALIZE the business engagement model.

FIGURE 6: Stage 2, Maturity of Business Process Transformation

6

What's Wrong with Driving Only Efficiency in Business Processes?

> **KEY INSIGHT:** It is possible to unintentionally focus too much on business process efficiency. When that happens, the effectiveness of the business operation suffers.

The previous trio of chapters on Stage 1 or *default* process transformation maturity described how efficiency can always be improved. Efficiency can be further enhanced by being more attuned to open market forces (as in Poste Italiane's story), driving E2E process accountability (as illustrated by the MH370 case), and creating *Dynamic Operating Engines* (as with the Ford turnaround situation). But focusing business operations on efficiency alone has obvious drawbacks. There are additional opportunities for business process effectiveness, innovation, and leadership. We will elaborate on these as we discuss the next three stages of maturity. In the next section, we offer an example of a business process that was so focused on improving efficiency that it became painful to its end customers. One such customer was Filippo, who will recount his experiences.

The Story: A Proven Business Process Suddenly Goes Sour

I (Filippo) have a memorable story that is relevant to this chapter. Unfortunately, it is memorable for all the wrong reasons. But the anecdote has generated good watchouts regarding the pitfalls of focusing process improvements solely on efficiency.

To start with, very few people like the hassle of packing and unpacking and the dozens of individually painful activities that are involved in moving. And the troubles get exponentially bigger if you're moving between countries. I am fortunate enough to have a family that was adventurous and supportive in packing up and moving to yet another country every time Procter & Gamble offered me a new assignment. Between 1989 and 2001 my family and I relocated internationally four times. And while the experience can never be called delightful, these moves went remarkably smoothly thanks to generous P&G support. However, the relocation in 2001 from the United States to Greece, which took place after P&G established a Global Business Services (GBS) organization, was distinctly memorable…because it was difficult. It felt as though my wife and I were managing a complex project involving dozens of suppliers, none of whom ever spoke to the others to coordinate even simple activities. It was a drastically different experience from previous relocations. How had this challenging but manageable process turned monstrously complicated so quickly? The answer to that is important in our journey from Stage 1 transformation for efficiency to Stage 2 transformation for effectiveness.

For context, any relocation is inherently very complicated. You need to dispose of your old house and cars, buy or rent new ones, arrange for packers, sign up for utilities, and so on. If you have a family, then changing schools may be necessary. Perhaps the spouse needs to change jobs. Now, take all that and add an international angle: visa applications, different languages, different educational systems, new types of appliances, splitting your goods into air shipment for immediate necessities and sea shipment for bulk goods. And a dozen other challenges. I had experienced that many times already, so my expectations were appropriately modest. Yet the move to Greece ended up being extremely complicated. To explain why, it is necessary to briefly describe how international relocations work in most multinational companies.

How Do International Relocations Work?

If a company needs to relocate an executive overseas for a few years, it can assist the employee and their family in several possible ways. It may pay for a decision-making trip regarding the assignment. It will hire several agencies ranging from visa specialists to others who manage packing and transportation of goods. It may hire realtors in the sending and receiving countries to organize for housing. Depending on the HR policies, other agencies may be provided for language lessons, school admissions for children, and so on.

To coordinate among all these agencies, the HR department in each country often has a few local vendors with whom they have established contracts. The employee being transferred simply works with the local HR. The benefit of this approach is its relative simplicity. The HR people know the home company and may even know the employee personally. They know how to coordinate with the HR counterparts in the receiving country. They know the company policies regarding the move and can make decisions quickly if needed. It's a relatively simple and personalized experience. However, the downside of this design is that it is not scaled—that is, each country must set up this operation on its own, and the resulting HR function doesn't always have specialized travel and relocation expertise. Thus, it can be relatively expensive. The starting point for many companies is to make the relocation process more cost-efficient. In our *Dynamic Process Transformation* framework, that's a Stage 1 activity (i.e., efficient business processes).

To address this issue of efficiency, companies create relocation "shared services." This requires the consolidation of all relocation-related HR employees, vendor contracts, policies, and systems into one centralized operation. That can drive cost savings because it means there are fewer global vendors vying for much larger contracts. It also drives consistency in benefits across countries. It should also help bring in experts in fields such as visa arrangements and shipping. That was the situation at P&G while Filippo was still in Cincinnati prior to his relocation to Athens. But Stage 1, efficiency-only business processes have their limitations. And he ran into those when moving to Greece.

Filippo's US-to-Greece International Relocation Experience Goes Sour

From Filippo's perspective as the employee being transferred, the relocation process had become very complex because a shared services structure had been created. To start with, the initial chat across the desk with the local HR relocation manager had been replaced by a comprehensive email listing all the steps in the process. That's fine, Filippo thought to himself—this is not ideal from an experience perspective, but it's still manageable. However, what followed was a lesson in what can go wrong when business processes deliver efficiency at the expense of effectiveness.

In pursuit of the best cost and service, P&G had added several specialized vendors to the mix. They were probably among the best in the world, but each was responsible for only a narrow part of the relocation (local trucking, international shipping, visas, customs, realtors, and so on). Each had a very formal and comprehensive form to capture Filippo's information. Each also had a very well-intentioned "single point of contact" who would work with him and his family. The specialized vendors were not required to share all the information with one another. You can see where this is headed.... Because it meant filling out a dozen comprehensive templates with repetitive information (names, addresses, passport details, itineraries, etc.) and coordinating with a dozen "single points of contact," this became painful quite quickly. And it became worse when something went wrong.

Clearly, this process had turned out to be the opposite of what it was originally intended to be. A well-intentioned network of best-in-class vendors collectively ended up delivering an international relocation process of poor effectiveness. This was obviously very disappointing for all organizations concerned. They were all high-quality teams, but pieced together, the results were disappointing for both the employees who used the service and for P&G itself.

Then, two years later, the situation got even worse!

P&G's International Relocation Process Gets Worse

Two years later, in 2003, P&G outsourced two-thirds of its Global Business Services (GBS) operations to HP, IBM, and Jones Lang LaSalle. Among the many outsourced services was a relatively small one, the international relocation service within HR. In the months and years following the outsourcing, things got much worse. By this time, Filippo had been appointed global head of GBS. International relocation services within GBS would become one of his biggest challenges.

Here's what happened. A couple of years earlier, when Filippo experienced the complex, siloed service in moving from the United States to Greece, the focus on efficiency had already created significant seams among the many services needed to deliver international relocations. Then P&G outsourced most of this work to a global vendor. This global outsourcing partner in turn had to employ other specialized companies for transportation carriers, visas, local real estate, and so on. The silos that had existed previously got even worse, because many of those silos were now part of different vendor companies. As a result, the international relocation process became even more unacceptable. In 2001, when Filippo moved to Greece, the poor results affected mostly the employee concerned. In 2003, after outsourcing, the poor results also affected the P&G business as well as the vendor businesses. The unfortunate process design meant that some critical expat executive assignments were delayed. Furthermore, some of the participating vendors lost money as they overspent to overcome process design faults. In this way, one of the smallest services within GBS became for a time one of the biggest headaches.

GBS set up a high-priority program to systemically address these issues. It redesigned the international relocation services end-to-end. Some of the services that had been outsourced were brought back in-house. Vendors were changed where appropriate. The international relocation services now had a new set of performance metrics that included both efficiency and effectiveness. As part of end-to-end management, GBS appointed single leaders responsible for the service. The results would become a model for other companies to apply to their own relocation services.

The effects of situations where efficiency-alone gets driven off the cliff can be painful to both the company and the person being relocated. We can apply these lessons in the Stage 2 *Open Market Rules* model, to prevent such failures.

The Learning:
Focus on Efficiency Alone Has Unintended Negative Implications

There are a couple of very valuable lessons from this story.

1. The efficiency-focused process during Filippo's relocation negatively impacted customer experience.

Just before Filippo relocated to Greece in 2001, the coordination work of the previous HR relocation experts had been distributed to the employee being relocated and to the relocation agencies. That may have created efficiency gains on paper, but it also created new process issues. This type of "efficiency-only" situation is more common than we might imagine. For instance, we see this in customer support. Call center services across industries have evolved over time, from onshore to offshore to mostly automated. In the process, some of them have become virtually inaccessible or have lost their human touch. Some have proved to be difficult to interact with or simply ineffective at answering queries and solving problems.

As a result, whatever cost efficiencies are gained are traded off against worse customer experience and satisfaction. To be fair, this focus on efficiency is a logical one for most businesses when they are faced with a need to reduce costs. All the examples mentioned earlier—standardizing, automating, offshoring, outsourcing, and so on—are proven methods to reduce costs. They do work. Except that there's a limit to how well these "efficiency-alone" solutions can work before they start to hurt overall business process *effectiveness*. The learning from this is that we must ensure that process *efficiency* gains are delivered along with process *effectiveness*, which must be equal to or higher than in the past.

2. The international relocation process after the outsourcing delivered even less business value because it was out of sync with the open market.

Two years after Filippo's relocation, when the work was outsourced, the process for international relocations had become so siloed that business results were impacted. Also, as mentioned earlier, the vendors themselves lost money, for they had to add staff to manually cope with a suboptimally designed process. The process design was poor. Worse, the global vendor that managed all relocation services was new to the process. It had in turn outsourced specific tasks to a bevy of specialized vendors in different countries. The costs of coordination across these were significant. Furthermore, the process management, process design, and governance work had also been partly delegated to the global vendor. In hindsight, P&G should have retained this work. In fact, the entire design for outsourcing management of the process was not in line with what the open market supported. True, it had been intended to be a cutting-edge design, but the lesson is that there's a difference between a new design that can be supported by the marketplace and one that is not based on market capabilities. All of this was fixed later as part of the new international relocations design.

The following model for *Open Market Rules* for Stage 2 addresses both the issues listed above (i.e., the customer experience problems and the business results).

The Model: *Open Market Rules* for Stage 2

The learning from the international relocation story illustrates the pitfalls of unbalanced approaches to process improvement. Pushing cost efficiencies at the expense of customer experience, or separately from the overall business value, is a mistake. Fortunately, there are a couple of simple principles, supported by clear action items, which can help avoid that mistake.

1. **Seek to increase customer experience when driving efficiency-seeking process transformations.**

Keep customer-experience key performance indicators (KPIs) in mind even when driving efficiency-related changes to processes. In today's world, seeking efficiency with unclear customer KPIs is a mistake— not just because the customer is important, but also because today's digital capabilities can deliver both together. Here are a few action items that facilitate this:

a. Ensure that process KPIs are measured E2E and that customer KPIs increase.

b. Use specialized tools such as *customer journey maps* to deliberately design the customer experience. We do not want customer experience to be an unplanned consequence of the process change. We want it to be thought of up-front as part of the whole business value.

c. Ensure that your process organization design allows for E2E process excellence as well as E2E customer support. Siloed organizational designs are a killer.

d. Leverage newer technology platforms that are designed for E2E process management rather than siloed. Many such platforms can also resolve problems across multiple systems.

2. **Design processes to capture both efficiency and effectiveness in business value, in keeping with the open market.**

It's important to avoid assuming that if processes are made efficient, then increased business value will follow. As the P&G international relocations example illustrates nicely, simply stringing together a bunch of siloed efficiency gains may not end up increasing business value. In fact, it may detract from overall business value if the new process design itself is suboptimized or in conflict with open market conditions.

Here are the action steps for designing and capturing full business value at this stage of maturity:

a. Use a process design approach that maximizes business value. Tools like process mapping, value stream analysis, and loss analysis do a better job than others of linking process designs to business outcomes.

b. Assign E2E process owner roles to ensure that business value is delivered even after the transformation project ends. We will elaborate on how to use product management principles to create these E2E ownership roles in Chapter 7.

c. Report performance results regularly and completely, based on what the business deems relevant. Begin to distinguish between clients and users. Clients are senior stakeholders who ultimately "pay" for the service and who are empowered to make choices about service levels. Users are the employees who use the service and have input as to what is an acceptable level of service. We will explain and elaborate on this in subsequent chapters.

d. Get more granular on the costs and benefits of processes. When transforming processes, become more precise in understanding the costs of the whole business process, the unit cost of each service item consumed, and the quantified benefits to each stakeholder organization.

In Closing

The above two principles of always seeking improved customer experience and being deliberate about capturing the business value of both efficiency and effectiveness go a long way toward codifying business process maturity. More importantly, they avoid the pitfalls of following efficiency-seeking ideas off the cliff. There are further insights and models for delivering process effectiveness value. We examine the use of the driver of *Unified Accountability* in the next chapter.

Checklist Items for Stage 2, *Open Market Rules*

To further strengthen your *Open Market Rules*, compare performance with the following Stage 2 characteristics:

- ☑ Processes need to be designed to deliver customer effectiveness, not just operations efficiency, and to eliminate seams and handoffs.

- ☑ Focus more strongly on making all the business associates (beyond process operations) more effective by freeing up their time and eliminating unnecessary touch points.

- ☑ Performance measures include customer value, as deemed important by the customer; these may range from ease of use to better experience and new capabilities.

- ☑ Users' and stakeholders' feedback must be carefully thought through to get actionable input; its relevance should be regularly reviewed and aligned with the business.

- ☑ Disciplined metrics must be designed to measure and report full business value; these should relate to efficiency, effectiveness, and innovation.

7

Applying Product Management to Business Processes

> **KEY INSIGHT:** You can apply product management practices to running business processes, thus making them more customer-centric and increasing accountability for performance.

We have all probably had the less than delightful experience of being repeatedly transferred from one department to another while trying to get something done. Perhaps this was in the context of an insurance claim, a vendor payment, or something else. Eventually, we get to the point of just asking to be escalated to the person in charge. In cases like these, we are seeking the person who is ultimately accountable to solve our problem. Pinning down accountability for outcomes is a common challenge in business processes. We will need to solve it as a part of our journey from Stage 1 (efficient) to Stage 2 (effective) business processes. Many times over the years, the authors have had the occasion to ponder this issue of process accountability. How do we systemically design for it? Conducting an end-to-end process redesign is only part of the answer. Doing so streamlines the steps in the business process but doesn't solve the organizational issue of who is ultimately accountable.

This quest for an organizational construct to strengthen accountability for E2E process results led us to examine the role of product managers. In the product world (e.g., an iPhone), the product manager is the person who is ultimately accountable for all aspects of performance, from financial to product quality to execution. The question that struck us was, *why can't we apply product management disciplines to internal company services, as in business processes?* Turns out, we can! More interestingly, it became evident that both of us had done just that during our time in Procter & Gamble's Global Business Services (GBS). We did it unconsciously, since product management—which is called brand management in P&G—had long been embedded in our DNA. Focusing on single accountability, understanding consumers, creating distinctive brands, and writing simple but memorable messaging had become second nature by the time we created the GBS model. Product management provided an organizing model that brought together resources from different organizations and enabled them to focus single-mindedly on the customer and the service "product."

Our act of subliminally transferring the product manager model to internal business processes was only appropriate, since the concept of product management itself originated with a P&G manager named Neil McElroy in 1931. Let's dive into McElroy's story to look for lessons we can reapply to Stage 2 maturity as we seek to strengthen *Unified Accountability* for process management.

The Story of Neil McElroy and the Invention of Brand Management

Neil Hosler McElroy is probably best known for being Secretary of Defense under President Eisenhower from October 9, 1957, to December 1, 1959.[22] He was incredibly prolific, though—he created the format of soap operas for television, helped found NASA, and gave birth to the idea of brand management. McElroy graduated from Harvard in 1925 as an economics major and began work in the advertising department of Procter & Gamble. He became vice president of advertising and promotion in 1943 and rose to become president of the company in 1948.

In 1931 McElroy wrote a famous three-page memo[23] that laid out the need to hire a couple of people as "Brand Men." These people would

Some of the World's Most Famous Entrepreneurs Were Also Great Product Managers

Jeff Bezos, Steve Jobs, Bill Gates, Michael Dell, Larry Page, Walt Disney, and Michele Ferrero (founder of the Ferrero chocolate firm) have founded some of the most successful companies in the world. They have a few things in common. None of them went to business school. All of them were masters of understanding needs in an underserved market. And all were masters at applying an emerging technology to solve customer problems. In today's world, these would be the role and skills of a product manager (i.e., identifying product opportunity, establishing product strategy, defining the product, and championing the product's use).

In recent years, product manager roles have exploded in importance and popularity. In its list of the 50 best jobs in America in 2021, Glassdoor ranked the role of product manager at #3. What's driving this demand is an appreciation that a disciplined approach to rapidly distilling unmet needs, and then turning them into delightful products, is a winning formula. The aforementioned entrepreneurs possessed great empathy for the customer, insights into what was possible, and the ability to distinguish between what was essential and what was incidental. They had a deep understanding of the customer as well as of their own team's capabilities. They operated from a strong basis of knowledge and confidence. And they created disruptively winning products as a result. That's why product management is exploding in importance in today's customer-centric business world.

be totally responsible for a specific brand, from tracking sales to managing the product, advertising, and promotions. They would attend to one brand and one alone (first up would be Ivory soap). The brand manager would understand the product's customer deeply and be wholly responsible for all the product's results. This single focus would ensure that the brand (and eventually other brands in the company by extension) would be marketed as if it were an all-inclusive business. This structure led to decentralized decision-making, which allowed critical decisions to be delegated as business grew.

How Brand Management Evolved Across Industries

Brand and product management transformed the consumer goods industry starting in the 1930s. Even if the idea had been restricted to that one industry, it would have been a big achievement; but the concept spread and evolved across industries over time. Author Martin Eriksson has mapped the penetration of McElroy's "Brand Men" idea into various industries such as computer hardware, motor cars, consumer electronics, and, more recently, software development.

While McElroy was advising at Stanford, he influenced two young entrepreneurs named Bill Hewlett and David Packard, founders of Hewlett-Packard. They interpreted the Brand Man ethos as putting decision-making as close as possible to the customer. In the seminal book *The Hewlett-Packard Way*, this policy is credited with sustaining Hewlett-Packard's 50-year record of unbroken 20% year-on-year growth between 1943 and 1993.

Meanwhile, as Martin Eriksson's work has demonstrated, in post-war Japan shortages and cash flow problems forced industries to develop just-in-time manufacturing. Taiichi Ohno and Eiji Toyoda (the nephew of Toyota's founder and eventually chief executive and chairman of Toyota Motor) took this idea and ran with it, developing the Toyota Production System and the Toyota Way over 30 years of continuous improvement. The focus was not just on eliminating waste in the production process, but also on two important principles that any modern product manager will recognize: Kaizen—improving the business continuously while always driving for innovation and evolution; and Genchi Genbutsu—going to the source to find the facts to make correct decisions.

When just-in-time came to the West, HP was among the first to embrace it. Then, as HP alumni spread throughout Silicon Valley, they took the concept to pretty much all hardware and software companies. Throughout this evolution, the product manager role would weave together the "marketing mix" responsibilities (product, place, price, promotion) with the product value proposition and product development.

In 2001, product management would metamorphosize into agile software development. Seventeen software engineers got together at a ski resort in Utah and wrote the Agile Manifesto. For software developers this was a watershed moment.

(Continued on next page)

> No longer were software developers merely mechanical programmers churning out exactly what was specified (regardless of whether the specs were appropriate); now their focus was on quick and iterative product development and working directly with customers.
>
> Interestingly, Agile and the just-in-time models of lean startup and lean enterprise are now closing the loop by returning to consumer goods product development.

Based on the success of the Ivory soap business, Richard Deupree, P&G's president, would expand the brand management structure until it replaced the previous functional model. In later years, almost every CEO at P&G after Deupree would have a strong background in brand management.

After World War II, brand management and its attendant decentralized structure penetrated most corporations, including General Motors under Alfred Sloan. Over the years, brand management continued to evolve. It would combine with the Toyota Way and would lead to a revolution in product management at Hewlett-Packard. More recently, its offshoots have been as varied as Agile Software Development and Lean Startup.

Learning from the McElroy Story for Stage 2 *Unified Accountability*

McElroy's original idea of dedicated accountability for each brand, and of enabling every brand to constantly evolve, is totally applicable to business processes as well. Recall that early in this book we mentioned that the biggest challenge with business processes over time is obsolescence. Processes get calcified and rigid even while the surrounding business environment evolves more quickly. Product managers can help with that issue too, in addition to solving the process accountability one.

We call this "service management," rather than "product management," because internal business processes are services rather than physical products. What the former has in common with the latter is the importance of running each business process as if it were an independent business. At first blush this may seem overly sophisticated, given that there may well be hundreds of business processes in an organization. Actually, our experience has been that this approach drives role clarity and focus, and generates fewer seams across organizations, all with very little overhead.

To run business processes as if they were independent businesses, at a minimum we will need to organize those processes into some coherent catalog and to be clear about the value proposition of each process; we will also need a methodology to create the ongoing strategy and actions to run each process as a business. The equivalent of these, in the *Dynamic Process Transformation* model, is as follows:

- Organizing structure for business processes → Service Catalog (Product Catalog)
- Value proposition of each process → Service Value Proposition (Product Value)
- Execution methodology → Service Management Framework (Brand Building Framework)

This *Unified Accountability* model for Stage 2 maturity integrates these three learnings to codify an approach for service management excellence.

The Model: Applying Product Management to Business Processes

The role of a service manager (i.e., the product manager role applied to processes) is to deliver stronger *Unified Accountability*. This is in terms of process operations results as well as for the sake of keeping processes relevant long-term. The three previous bullet points apply here too.

1. Create a business processes service catalog.

You might wonder why we need to create a catalog of services. After all, most organizations can list off their functions and processes (finance, HR, etc., as functions; and record-to-report, procure-to-pay, etc., as processes). There are two reasons why—to strengthen accountability for each item in the catalog and to reduce process overlaps. The first one is intuitive, so let's talk about the second, using the example of payroll. In some organizations, for historical reasons, there may be multiple payroll processes. We would want to harmonize these over time. Also, it's possible that there are differences in the scope of the payroll processes themselves (e.g., one business includes benefits management within the payroll process, while another one doesn't). A process catalog brings these important variations to the surface. It also facilitates assigning accountability to address them.

Interestingly, this rationale for creating a formal service catalog isn't too different from what initially drove McElroy to the idea of brand management. His 1931 "Brand Men" memo was inspired by his dissatisfaction with the marketing of somewhat overlapping soap brands at the time at Procter & Gamble—Ivory and Camay.[24] While working on the advertising campaign for Camay, McElroy became frustrated with having to compete not only with soaps from Lever and Palmolive, but also with Ivory, P&G's own flagship product. In his famous memo, he argued that more concentrated attention should be paid to Camay, and by extension to other P&G brands as well. In other words, he sought to create a structure in which each brand would have a distinct position in the product hierarchy.

Note that McElroy wasn't advocating for one of the two brands to be eliminated, but for the two brands to be distinguished from each other. Similarly, when applying the product catalog concept to business processes (i.e., when creating a service catalog), the goal isn't necessarily to have one-size-fits-all services (e.g., only one payroll process for all business units); rather, it is to be clear on the distinctiveness of overlapping services.

Process Catalog: Equivalent to Product Catalog
(examples)

BUSINESS PRODUCT CATALOG	SERVICE CATALOG
Business Unit *Fabric & Home Care*	**Service Line** *Human Resources* *Processes Service Line*
Category *Laundry*	**Service Category** *Compensation & Benefits*
Brand *Tide*	**Service** *Payroll Services*
SKU *Tide Pods 64 pieces*	**Solution** *Time & Attendance*

FIGURE 7: Business Process Catalog

Once we start building up a service catalog for a given business process (e.g., compensation and benefits within HR), and, within it, the respective services (e.g., payroll within that), the parallel with the hierarchical design of a product catalog becomes evident. At the top of a hierarchy of business processes there is usually a broad end-to-end business process, which we refer to as a "service line," which is analogous to a business unit line. In Figure 7, we demonstrate this. All HR business processes could be viewed as being like an entire product category for a business process (e.g., Fabric and Home Care) in the figure.

Under the service line, one might have multiple service categories (compensation and benefits, talent acquisition, training, development, etc.). In the product catalog equivalent, you would find multiple product categories (Laundry, Dish Cleaning, etc.) The hierarchy would continue a few levels down, depending on the complexity of the product/service. Laying out a service catalog creates a distinctive map of business processes and drives the conversation for each service to be distinctive in creating value for the enterprise. The next step is to go deeper and identify the value proposition of each individual service.

2. Define a clear service value proposition.

Brand value propositions speak to our audience clearly regarding the distinctive need they can meet. Walmart promises that we can buy the things we need at the best prices. Amazon offers the ultimate online store—buy anything, anytime, easily. Intuit (maker of TurboTax, Quick-Books, and Mint) offers the value proposition of smart and simple-to-use accounting software for small businesses and individuals. Each of these brands strives to live up to its brand equity in all its activities. They promise something that stands out from their competitors in meeting consumer needs.

In the world of business processes, there is a real risk that this mind-set is lacking. After all, if our function was created to perform very specific tasks (e.g., run payroll at the lowest cost and best service levels possible), then it seems unnecessary to even define a service value proposition. After all, our job is to deliver payroll activities, and we are going to do that no matter what it takes. We are going to hound employees to hand in their time and attendance sheets, where relevant, so that we can run the payroll on time. We are going to incrementally improve service quality and cost year on year, but we are not going to invest too much into innovation that might disrupt weekly or monthly payroll services. The risk is that we underperform on consumer needs and consumer understanding. Or that we focus continuous improvement only on cost while ignoring other user-experience possibilities or innovative ideas. Why would we need to imagine payroll being turned into a delightful consumer-oriented payment service like PayPal or Venmo?

Most service-oriented businesses have a straightforward equation for defining the value proposition (see Figure 8). The numerator is a combination of benefits, including functional benefits (such as service quality), experiential benefits (such as user delight), and business outcome benefits (innovative models that deliver value beyond the narrow service). Expedia, AirBnB, and Uber are good illustrations of this model, in that they build in experiential benefits and smaller innovations to

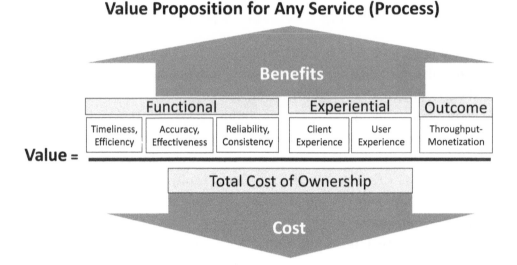

FIGURE 8: Business Process Value Proposition

complement service quality benefits. Also, the denominator is more sophisticated than the average "cost" measure. It accounts for "total cost of ownership," that is, for all types of costs that go into delivering the service (e.g., the time wasted by users if service quality is poor).

Once our service has a distinctive place in a service catalog and a clearly identified value proposition, it is time to run the service "as a business" by applying an execution methodology. The one below is based on the bedrock of P&G's brand management model—the "Brand Building Framework."

3. Use a disciplined service management framework.

The third step in running processes as products is to approach the execution of service operations in the same manner that one might deal with brand execution. Neil McElroy's approach toward running each brand as if it was an independent business has evolved over the past nine decades into a proven formula used by all P&G brands. It is called the Brand Management Framework, and it uses a set of questions to build a strong product or service (see Figure 9). The Brand Building Framework (BBF) places the customer at the heart of the process. To

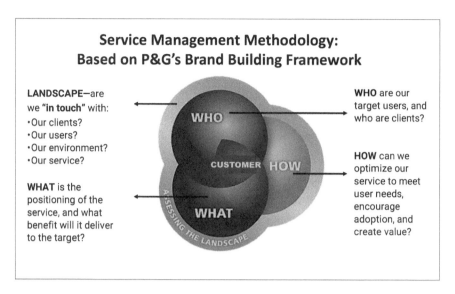

Service Management Methodology: Based on P&G's Brand Building Framework

LANDSCAPE–are we **"in touch"** with:
• Our clients?
• Our users?
• Our environment?
• Our service?

WHAT is the positioning of the service, and what benefit will it deliver to the target?

WHO are our target users, and who are clients?

HOW can we optimize our service to meet user needs, encourage adoption, and create value?

FIGURE 9: Brand Building Framework

delight the customer consistently, four steps are employed. The implementation of these steps in the context of our Stage 2 *Unified Accountability* model goes as follows.

a. Assess the LANDSCAPE for the service offering.

Understand the 360-degree context of the business process. This includes conducting a deep examination of the users (those who use the services), the clients (those who foot the bill), and the environment in which we operate, as well as acquiring a deep understanding of the current state of the service itself. Very few business process owners allow themselves the opportunity to do a periodic review of their service's landscape in any depth. For most organizations, running daily operations leaves little room for disciplined strategy renewal. That's in stark contrast to the well-organized strategy assessment that product leaders do periodically.

b. Understand the WHO.

Next, segment the types of users for each process. For example, the admin assistant who actually keys in the manager's travel expense report has different needs than the manager. There's often a dynamic tension between users and clients. Users may love to get delightful service without significant thought about its cost, while clients (executives who foot the bill as payers, as part of an accounting cross-charge) may be motivated to balance cost and service levels. Understanding our clients and doing further segmentation among them becomes critical.

c. Understand the WHAT.

Identify exactly *what* we'd like our service to stand for. In other words, what is the positioning of the service, what do we want its image to be among users, and what benefit will it deliver to the target users? Part of this entails strategic decision-making (i.e., What do we want our service to be?). The other part is communications planning (i.e., Can we succinctly and clearly articulate its brand equity?).

d. Understand the HOW.

Once the three previous steps of *landscape, who,* and *what* are completed, it's time to decide *how* the service will be delivered. The parallel to the world of product management is with the old 4 Ps of marketing.

- Service design and operation (Product)
- Coverage and adoption (Place)
- Communications (Promotion)
- Cost budgeting and allocation strategy (Price)

In summary, this methodology of creating a service catalog, defining clear value propositions for each service, and using a professional service management model provides the discipline necessary to mature our processes to Stage 2. By being clear about our offerings, by being intentional when designing the value they must address, and by using a disciplined methodology to deliver accountability in outcomes, we reduce the risk of process obsolescence.

In Closing

Running business processes as if they were independent businesses simply reapplies what has been acknowledged over nine decades when it comes to product management, which is the need to have dedicated resources that are accountable so as to focus on winning on each brand. In our case we reapplied from brand management to win in service management. Taking a disciplined approach to rapidly distill core unmet needs, and then turning service management iteratively into delightful products or services, has been highly effective. As we further strengthen the process maturity at Stage 2, we start to look at factors beyond methodologies—specifically, behaviors in the organization that further facilitate effectiveness (see the next chapter).

Checklist Items for Stage 2, *Unified Accountability*

To strengthen *Unified Accountability*, compare performance with the following Stage 2 characteristics:

- ☑ Processes are run as "products," with centralized accountability; there is great consistency in the skill set and tools being applied.

- ☑ Service managers have been appointed to run processes end-to-end and holistically: cost, feedback, KPIs, quality, and ongoing transformation.

- ☑ A process catalog has been defined, bringing strong transparency and clarity to the users and stakeholders.

- ☑ There is absolutely no confusion about who is in charge, and empowered, to drive continuous improvement in the individual processes.

- ☑ Each process has a well-articulated and aligned-to value proposition; this makes the interaction between operations and the business extremely clear and productive.

8

Achieving Transparency in Business Processes

> **KEY INSIGHT:** Transparency in business processes is a powerful strategy. It fosters collaboration and systemically accelerates process effectiveness.

As business processes become increasingly mature in efficiency and effectiveness, the question becomes this: Is there a model to codify the organizational behaviors related to effectiveness?

There is. It involves creating a *Dynamic Operating Engine* based on transparency. Strategically using transparency in business processes is a big idea. It acts as an accelerant for alignment and collaboration. Interestingly, transparency as a strategy is not new. It has proved itself as a business model in several product organizations. The most noteworthy of these is the American apparel company, Patagonia. Let's dig into their story to sift for lessons for business process effectiveness.

The Story: Transparency as a Business Model at Patagonia

Would you put out a full-page advertisement in the *New York Times*, on the most important retail sales day of the year, telling your audience *not* to buy your product? Fashion brand Patagonia did just that on Black Friday in 2011,[25] in a campaign labeled "Don't Buy This Jacket." It took this unusual step after an internal sustainability audit uncovered that some of its suppliers were subjecting workers to deplorable conditions, including making them pay thousands of dollars just to work. It wasn't an advertising gimmick; it is very much at the core of the company's culture and business model. As its founder Yvon Chouinard has said, "I know it sounds crazy, but every time I've made a decision that's best for the planet, I've made money."

Patagonia is the gold standard for brands living out their values and purpose. In 2022, Chouinard announced that he would give away his company to fight climate change. In founding Patagonia, Chouinard always wanted to deliver more than just climbing equipment. He was seeking to alleviate problems within the climbing world and to do good for the environment at the same time. Decades of pioneering work in environmental activism and in the responsible use of materials in production have done exactly that. The company now operates 100% renewable electricity across its US-based facilities and 76% globally.[26] It's on the way to reaching net-zero, which includes zero waste to landfill by 2025. That's a tough goal in the apparel industry, where old clothing ends up in landfill; then add to that the issue of carbon-intensive supply chains. Patagonia has committed to recycle every product and byproduct of its business.[27]

However, in addition to Patagonia's purpose-driven work on sustainability, it is its culture of transparency that's worth noting. That includes its unprecedented openness to acknowledging problems within the company. That's remarkable in the current world, where widespread greenwashing, spin, and outright lying aren't uncommon. On the heels of the UN climate summit in Glasgow (COP26), Patagonia published an article in *Fortune* mentioning that it doesn't use the word "sustainable" because it recognizes that it is part of the problem. That's a remarkable start.[28] Furthermore, it has used transparency as a rallying cry for the entire industry. It has used its goal of net-zero by 2025 as a call for help from other industry partners. Patagonia reported in the same *Fortune* article that "the biggest problem here is that 95% of our emissions come from our supply chain, and we are a minor

Benefits of Transparency as a Business Model

The trend toward transparency as a business model has accelerated in recent times. In online review sites and discussion forums, businesses are being held much more accountable for their claims, their operations, and their impact on the world. In response, organizations face the choice between playing defense (doing the minimum, spinning their results, etc.) or going on the offense (i.e., embracing transparency). Patagonia and others have demonstrated that there are tangible reasons to choose the latter path. Transparency fosters trust, collaboration, and better operational performance.

T-Mobile is an example of using transparency to build trust—which includes *regaining* customers' trust after a major outage. In the fall of 2015, when faced with the Experian data breach, the T-Mobile CEO, John Legere, immediately used his own social media account to respond to individual customer questions. While the breach was not T-Mobile's fault, Legere accepted the responsibility of informing and reassuring customers, besides providing resources to monitor and manage any potential problems.

An example of transparency to facilitate collaboration is Patagonia's offer to let smaller brands use its factories; in this way it helped fund the "greening" of the supply chain.

And then there's transparency as a strategy to improve performance. This emerged in 1993 at Bridgewater Associates. Company founder Ray Dalio was seeking ways to improve the company's performance and hit upon the idea of a culture of openness as a competitive advantage. The version that emerged is called radical transparency—everyone knows everything about everyone. It is effective, though not always easy. It has worked for Bridgewater Associates, which grew from being a startup in Dalio's New York apartment in 1975 to becoming one of the world's largest hedge fund management companies.

player on this stage. We are developing an 'insetting' approach in our supply chain by setting up a joint funding mechanism where other smaller brands can partner with us to invest in 'greening' the factories. As is the case for many of our progressive ideas, we currently have only a hunch that it will work, but we know we have to try."

Patagonia has proved that purpose and transparency can be profitable. The company has inspired outstanding brand loyalty, delivered remarkable financial performance, and gained global sustainability recognition, including the prestigious UN Champion of the Earth award.[29] Beyond its purpose-driven work, it has proved that embracing a culture of openness, humility, and systemic change is a force multiplier. In our work to keep growing business process maturity, there are lessons to be learned from transparency as a strategy. It is a lever that can align business process customers and suppliers, foster an open environment of collaboration, and create a virtuous circle of a culture of ongoing improvement. Creating such a transparency-based *Dynamic Operating Engine* is the focus of the rest of this chapter.

Lessons from Patagonia on Using Transparency in Operations

Transparency builds trust, collaboration, and performance. It all starts with a foundation of credible messaging—something that product and process managers would love to strengthen. Patagonia's legions of loyal customers trust the company implicitly. The "Don't Buy This Jacket" ad strengthened the public's conviction that this was a highly ethical company. On collaboration, Patagonia's transparency regarding the challenges of "greening" the apparel industry supply chain, and its invitation to other companies to work with it, is another excellent example. And in terms of performance, Patagonia's strong financial results underlie other important findings—for example, that customers are willing to try out more premium products. Beyond the anecdotal experience of companies, there is study data that organizations and employees perform better in transparent conditions. Studies in neuroscience have underscored that our brains work best when we no longer feel the need to hide, cover up our mistakes, or dwell on errors.[30]

Clearly, transparency is a powerful strategy. It can strengthen trust, collaboration, and performance systemically as part of the *Dynamic Operating Engine,* and in our own experience it works extremely well. Having studied this issue at length, we believe that transparency works so well for business processes because it tears down the veil to the backroom processes mystique. Let's face it, most employees in the organization have no need to understand the gory details of IT, finance, or supply chain processes. Certainly, we must not force this upon them, but we need to address the faulty assumption that these operations are not relevant to them—that being passive customers of the process is sufficient. The ball is in the court of the process organization to think through what information is relevant and, more importantly, what common goals are important to its customers.

We also know that process organizations continue to be on the defensive with trust, collaboration, and effectiveness. So the issue isn't *whether* to employ transparency as part of our *Dynamic Operating Engine,* but *how.* What exactly do we need to be more transparent about? And how do we avoid oversharing information with users and business partners? The good news is that we have strong data on how transparency can be employed. It needs to be used in cost, value, and KPI performance. We elaborate on these three items in the Stage 2 model for *Dynamic Operating Engine.*

The Model: Transparency in Business Processes

The context for this model is important. It is not as if most process organizations don't share information on cost, value, and KPI performance with other business partners. The issue is that the current information-sharing approaches are not effective. They don't address the basic reason *why* process organizations need to defend their cost, value, and KPIs more than others. Hence the trick here isn't to *start*

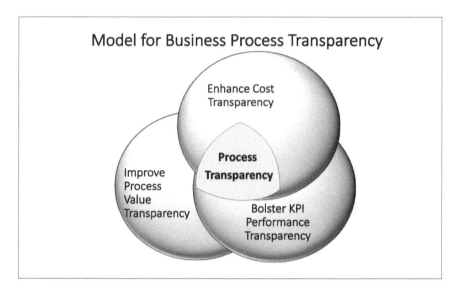

FIGURE 10: Drivers of Process Transparency

being transparent, but to get more sophisticated about it. Figure 10 depicts the three parts of the model.

1. Enhance process cost transparency by using "resource units."

The challenge for most process organizations regarding cost transparency is that too often their information is neither actionable nor meaningful enough. Let's illustrate this with an example, keeping in mind that the customer of this information is the senior corporate or business unit leader. Let's take a process such as PC support and assume that we already share a complete picture of all costs (cost of PC hardware, number and cost of employees working in this service, reliability of the service, etc.). Isn't that being transparent? The trouble is that while this is fine from an overall control perspective, it may not be meaningful or actionable enough. It is as if you as a customer of the electricity service at home are being given information on the costs of power generation, employee costs, and power supply reliability. That information is mostly irrelevant to the direct needs of customers. What's missing is the unit consumption cost information, which *is* actionable for them.

That's where the concept of "resource units" (RUs) comes in. An RU is a unit of consumption of a business process or service. You can define options with corresponding cost implications for each RU. So, going back to employee PC services, you might have different RU options for, say, a high-end laptop at a higher unit cost, and a lower-end option at a lower unit cost. Furthermore, you might have additional RUs for concierge PC support for key executives, versus self-support options for others, with different unit cost implications. Offering a handful of such RU options allows your process customers to make choices. In this case, you as the business unit leader could decide what level of services would be most appropriate for segments of your people, to optimize your costs.

Identifying actionable RUs helps incentivize the right behavior regarding the organization's business processes. However, the idea is not to offer choices willy-nilly. For instance, there may be nonnegotiable standards, such as those related to the use of a common Enterprise Resource Planning (ERP) system like SAP in the company. You don't need RU choices there. The intent is to enable the right behavior in the organization via actionable cost metrics.

The next level of sophistication in cost transparency involves sharing information about the context of these costs. How do they compare with open market costs? What is the E2E cost of a process for the company? So, for example, if we take a cross-functional process such as order-to-cash, would we be able to identify its true cost without engaging in too much financial gymnastics? The more our process cost information reflects business reality and actionability, the stronger the engagement and trust.

2. Improve transparency of processes by sharing the full value picture.

The second way to enhance transparency of processes is by being clear about their value. Every business process in the organization, whether it is maintaining financial books, processing customer orders, or paying employees, has some business value associated with it. Some processes may be considered the cost of doing business (e.g., payroll for employees), and others could have financial value directly attributable to the process (e.g., acquiring each new online customer).

The most common challenge with process value transparency has to do with measuring the value itself. Organizations often do a better job of identifying process costs than benefits. When value is being measured, another common trap is to equate process benefit with financial numbers only. Those are obviously crucial, but in many cases they may present an incomplete or, worse still, inaccurate picture of value. Three types of process value metrics are possible. A combination of all or some of them may be necessary to provide a holistic value picture.

a. **E2E financial value:** When it is possible to measure, this may be the best type of metric, but it doesn't need to be exclusive. Acquiring new customers, freeing up cash by reducing product inventory, reducing material procurement costs, and so on—each of these typically can be measured in terms of a financial benefit to the company. If a business process can be transformed to reduce the cost of operations, increase cash flow, or increase revenue, then capture a financial value metric. Avoid fuzzy monetary value metrics, or, if these are unavoidable, complement the picture with other firm financial value metrics. An example is "cost avoidance." This is an especially vexing challenge in processes like procurement. A good procurement deal is most likely going to avoid future costs, but the underlying assumptions regarding what cost saving will be accrued in the future can be tricky unless thoroughly validated. In this case, make sure it's formally vetted.

b. **Experiential value:** With the growing awareness of the value of user experience (UX), this is becoming an important complement to financial benefit reporting. This was always recognized as an external customer value metric for customer acquisition, retention, and leverage, but UX is now increasingly being appreciated as a core metric for internal company processes because of its implications for employee retention, motivation, and organizational culture. The use of the net promoter score (NPS) for internal business processes continues to expand. Other UX-related metrics are possible besides, such as these:

- Satisfaction scores, at the overall process *and* task levels
- Focus group ratings for detailed, qualitative feedback on experience
- Star ratings, especially for online reviews
- System usability scale (SUS), a common metric used by UX researchers and designers

c. **Process-agility-related value:** This important set of metrics is often overlooked. Measures of parameters such as speed to market, product development time, customer request turnaround, flexibility in manufacturing or logistics, sourcing and supplier flexibility, and so on, have assumed increased importance with the rise of nimble, digitally native competitors, as well as with the impact of the COVID-19 pandemic and other types of macroeconomic turmoil. In such environments, it is vital to examine the business value of process speed and flexibility.

3. Bolster KPI performance transparency by targeted KPI messaging.

Tracking operational metrics and reporting against service-level agreements should be a no-brainer. In reality, though, performance management reporting is half science (of measurement) and half art (of communication). That may sound like an exaggeration, but it isn't. The difficulty with KPI performance transparency is the same as with cost transparency—how is information to be made meaningful and actionable to the specific target audience? For the most effective KPI transparency, it is paramount to understand which stakeholders need to know what, and when. There is an art to doing this well, one that involves planning communications carefully rather than drawing up a distribution list for detailed KPIs as an afterthought.

The points being made here about applying formal marketing and communications methodologies in performance management aren't metaphorical—they are meant to be taken literally. Most business process performance reporting risks getting business leadership's attention only when something breaks: when a payroll is missed or a customer doesn't receive a shipment. Continuous business performance improvement is too often denied the opportunity to get the credit it deserves. If process operations are taken for granted, we lose the ability to engage the business on innovative interventions to deliver competitive advantage via business processes.

The recommended action step here is to approach KPI communication the same way a marketing person does a communications plan. Identify the various target audiences, list what each of them needs to know, and specify the communication medium to be used in each case (email, text, etc.). Be deliberate in planning the frequency of messaging. Disciplined KPI communication builds trust, and on that foundation, further collaboration and transformation can be supported.

In Closing

Being deliberate on how to leverage transparency to grow process maturity presents a potent opportunity. If it is built into the *Dynamic Operating Engine*, it pays dividends. This concludes our Stage 2 related models. At this stage, we have added customer value in addition to efficiency in Chapter 5, applied product management principles for *Unified Accountability* in Chapter 6, and, finally, added transparency to the *Dynamic Operating Engine* in this chapter. Put together, Stage 2 has made processes more effective and efficient. In the next stage, we up the ante by also delivering constant process innovation.

Checklist Items for Stage 2, *Dynamic Operating Engine*

To strengthen the *Dynamic Operating Engine*, compare performance with the following Stage 2 characteristics:

- ☑ Business operations are run with strong transparency, across all dimensions: cost, performance, and value.

- ☑ KPIs are based on business outcome and defined jointly with the stakeholders for maximum business relevance.

- ☑ Processes are constantly analyzed for improvement and/or transformation opportunities and to understand all aspects of cost.

- ☑ Process value is clearly articulated, with focus on the financial, experiential, and agility aspects of the process.

- ☑ Business processes are operated with the customer/stakeholder in mind. Their feedback is an integral part of the virtuous cycle. There is full transparency on how it influences operations.

PART IV

Stage 3 of Business Processes—
Integrated Maturity

Stage 3: Integrated Maturity. Focuses on Innovation

Action Steps for *Dynamic Process Transformation*

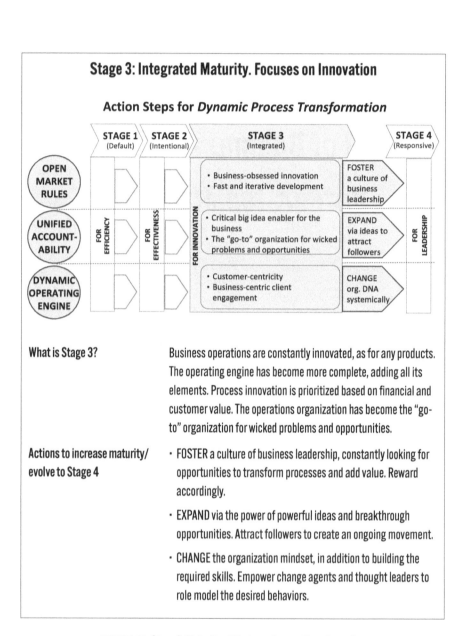

What is Stage 3?

Business operations are constantly innovated, as for any products. The operating engine has become more complete, adding all its elements. Process innovation is prioritized based on financial and customer value. The operations organization has become the "go-to" organization for wicked problems and opportunities.

Actions to increase maturity/ evolve to Stage 4

- FOSTER a culture of business leadership, constantly looking for opportunities to transform processes and add value. Reward accordingly.

- EXPAND via the power of powerful ideas and breakthrough opportunities. Attract followers to create an ongoing movement.

- CHANGE the organization mindset, in addition to building the required skills. Empower change agents and thought leaders to role model the desired behaviors.

FIGURE 11: Stage 3, Maturity of *Business Process Transformation*

9

Mastering Process Innovation

KEY INSIGHT: The potential for business process innovation is three times more than we think. Doing only continuous improvement on processes is insufficient.

Congratulations on moving up the process transformation maturity curve to Stage 3! By the end of the previous stage, you have highly efficient and effective business processes. Many companies stop there. They think, "After all, what problem are we trying to solve? Our processes are fine." That's a mistake. There is at least as much if not more value still to be unlocked from process transformation. The actual data from our experience at Procter & Gamble's GBS indicate that beyond efficiency and effectiveness, there is three times more business value at the next stages of maturity. This new value will not come from further streamlining, standardizing, and automating the process. To take an example, if we have already streamlined our road transportation logistics process, then further polishing it will not deliver three times the value. No, the new value will come from building upon that process. All the work done at the previous stages has provided us with a rich mine of data. And in today's world, where every company is a data company, this is gold. We can now start to reimagine logistics. Whether that's through drones, or new distribution centers, or new trucking partnerships, is the work of further innovation.

How to start unlocking this three-times value through relentless process innovation is the topic of the next trio of chapters. And as usual, we can look for insights and inspiration from parallel organizations. This time we look at one of the most innovative companies in the world—Amazon. The story of how it innovated to introduce free shipping offers plenty of insights.

How Amazon Innovated to Launch Free Shipping

Amazon Prime, the subscription service that offers free shipping, has been called the highest-grossing employee idea of all time.[31] It has more than 200 million subscribers and is available in more than 23 countries. The company generates more than $25Bn per year from Prime and other subscription services. Nine out of ten people get an Amazon Prime subscription because of its free shipping.[32] However, the innovation to make Prime a success had a slow start. It had more than its fair share of skeptics initially.

Prior to Prime, Amazon had launched Free Super Saver Shipping in January 2002. It didn't work as well as hoped, and Amazon feared that it would fall behind its rival, eBay. A team of Amazon employees came up with an idea for a membership club that would offer free two-day shipping. Prime, which launched in February 2005, was a first of its kind: for an upfront payment of $79, customers would receive unlimited free deliveries. And with that, Amazon would forever transform the way the world shops, raising the bar for convenience in online shopping.

However, the way this innovation evolved from 2005 to today provides some great lessons. The genesis of the formal proposal for Prime started with an Amazon engineer, Charlie Ward, who submitted the idea of offering unlimited "all-you-can-eat" type shipping.[33] Jeff Bezos took that a step further: he added the idea of *faster* shipping, in addition to *unlimited* shipping. Bezos has always espoused radical customer-centricity, and he believed that the idea of offering users a reason to stay and grow with Amazon was massive. He called in staff for a meeting at his boathouse on a Saturday amid a crazy holiday shopping period. Prime was conceived that day.

It wasn't all easy going for Prime. Since shipping was part of the profit margin for Amazon, this meant they took a financial hit. Several individuals inside the company feared that this could be the idea that sank the company. However, Prime would turn out to be a self-fulfilling prophecy. To help with the financial hit, Amazon would improve its logistics to reduce the amount of product it shipped by air. A couple of years after launch, Amazon established FBA (Fulfillment by Amazon), which allowed sellers to contract with Amazon to ship their products. This added further to the attractiveness of Prime for customers. A bit later, Prime Student was introduced, offering Prime free for a year to students. This would shape their online shopping behavior for a generation and more.

It would take Prime several years to truly take off. It wasn't until Prime Video was added as a free benefit to members in 2011 that it became a juggernaut. Then came Prime Music as a limited benefit. By 2014, Prime had snowballed sufficiently that Greg Greeley, VP of Prime, went to all business unit leaders within Amazon seeking agreement to add their services to Prime to systemically drive more engagement with Amazon customers. Once that tipping point was reached, there was no going back.

Of course, Prime is just one innovation example, and much has been written on what makes Amazon innovative. There's the concept of customer obsession, which goes way beyond customer-centricity. Then there's a culture of innovation at speed. And the willingness to sacrifice short-term financial results for long-term strategy. And, of course, there is the practice of considering ideas as assets. Some of these will no doubt be easier than others to reapply to process innovation. But the specific story of Prime has a rich offering of lessons for process innovation. Let's examine this further.

Lessons from Amazon Prime for *Open Market Rules* at Stage 3

At the Stage 3 level of maturity, the driver of *Open Market Rules* is all about bringing constant innovation to business processes. Among the many lessons the Amazon Prime story serves up, we'd like to highlight the three most relevant ones.

1. Embrace the divinely discontented customer.

It's true that the story of Prime offers a powerful example of customer-centricity. However, the learning goes way beyond customer-centricity and into customer obsession. Amazon goes several steps past delivering what its customers need, and adopts an opportunity mindset. It embraces the customer's fickle beliefs as opportunities for innovation. In his 2017 Letter to Shareholders,[34] Jeff Bezos called out the importance of staying on top of customers' ever-increasing expectations. "One thing I love about customers," Jeff wrote, "is that they are divinely discontent.... People have a voracious appetite for a better way, and yesterday's 'wow' quickly becomes today's 'ordinary.'" Embracing the conflict and complexity of the open market customer and distilling durable customer needs into a constant stream of innovations has certainly worked for Amazon.

Embracing the fickle and demanding customer as an innovation opportunity is very applicable to business processes as well. The work in *corporate* customer experience has been a step behind the discipline of *consumer* user experience. There's an opportunity to leapfrog by using the signals from divinely discontented corporate process customers as innovation opportunities. So, for instance, the user who chafes at submitting expense reports could be a trigger to eliminate expense reports entirely. Several companies have done so by resorting to AI to simulate an expense report, using corporate credit card data.

2. Connect the dots for potential solutions.

Prime was created out of new layers of free offerings over the years. What was constant over time was the goal of creating a moat around loyal customers so that they would never have to leave. However, the addition of each of the new, free services was highly opportunistic. Offering Prime Video for free to Prime members was initially puzzling even to some Amazon folks, as they questioned what video had to do with free shipping. It's a great example of connecting two seemingly unrelated dots for Amazon to meet its higher goal: a stronger customer moat.

3. Discipline in being fast and iterative.

When the concept for Prime was first discussed, Bezos was disciplined in setting the team an urgent but relevant deadline. The product would have to be announced in six weeks, on Amazon's Earnings Day.

This is very consistent with Amazon's overall philosophy on fast and iterative innovation. Its approach has customer obsession at the core. That is supported by leadership principles that guide day-to-day behavior, such as "Think Big," "Bias for Action," and "Frugality." And all of this is then brought to life by Amazon's toolbox of methodologies. Those tools are based on working backward from the customer benefit, all the way back to what needs to change at the starting point. This methodology of working backward permeates even routine operational processes such as budget management. When it comes to getting funding for work, the budget is simply an outcome of the plan for the work. In this way, planning and budgeting processes are combined. Most of the time is spent on the plan—the budget then follows.

That is in sharp contrast to the behaviors in most process organizations. For instance, in budgeting the process starts with the previous year's total and is then refined to incorporate productivity improvements. Discussion on innovation is most often a separate portfolio process. As a consequence, the chance to use financial processes to incentivize fast and iterative innovation is lost.

These three learnings—embracing the divinely discontented customer, connecting the dots on potential solutions, and discipline in fast and iterative innovation—have been incorporated into our model for process innovation.

The Model: Business-Value-Obsessed Process Innovation (BOPI)

As we apply the lessons from Prime, we need to note that the equivalent of the term "customer" at Amazon would include both the "user" and the "client" in the case of business processes. As mentioned earlier, they are both customers of business processes in their own right. We serve them both when we focus on delivering business value via processes. That is why we use the term "business-value obsession" rather than customer obsession. Essentially, business-value-obsessed process innovation is a model for delivering process innovation, based on embracing the divinely discontented customers, thus creating new business value. We will flesh out our model by elaborating on three action steps, linking them to the Prime lessons.

1. Embrace the divinely discontented user and client.

In the lessons from Amazon, we commented on how *customer obsession* goes a step beyond *customer-centricity*. In the process world, the reality is that most organizations are still at *customer satisfaction,* which is a step below *customer-centricity*. Here's what tends to happen. First, numeric customer satisfaction and user experience data are usually employed as the foundation for process management as well as innovation. The problem with numeric information is that it provides directional data but not the flavor and context needed for new innovations. At Amazon, mind-boggling amounts of data are available, yet anecdotes trump data. As Bezos has said, "The thing I have noticed is that when the anecdotes and the data disagree, the anecdotes are usually right. There is something wrong with the way that you are measuring it."

The indicated action in our BOPI model is to go beyond the numbers. We must smell and taste the opportunities. The best way to accomplish this is by embedding ourselves into the user and client organizations, or vice versa. The role of client manager, which we will detail in Chapter 11, helps us embed ourselves with clients. Similarly, the service manager role (see Chapter 7) enables focused and dedicated study of users.

2. Connect the dots for potential solutions.

It is interesting how many "connect the dots" ideas in the Prime story came from Bezos himself (e.g., his suggestion to add fast shipping to free shipping, or to bundle video into the Prime subscription). This capability is unique to certain individuals (Steve Jobs also had it). For most other situations, using a specific methodology to connect the dots can accomplish something similar. We believe that Design Thinking can be leveraged here. Design Thinking is a creative problem-solving process that is widely used by product and service organizations for innovation. As a process, it already has an advantage, because one of its steps is "customer empathy," which is incidentally the starting point of the entire Design Thinking process. Beyond that, it is during the step called "ideation" that it truly excels in connecting the dots. The exercise of "reframe the problem" facilitates defining the issue broadly enough that it opens up different possibilities for solutions. Design Thinking also offers exercises under "look for parallel problems" to cross-fertilize ideas from totally different contexts. For example, budgeting is a parallel to maintaining a diet.

Design Thinking can be useful not just in corporate innovation groups and in Silicon Valley startups, but also for routine ideation to improve, say, accounting operations or supply chain redesign.

3. Be disciplined in being fast and iterative.

The point was made earlier that customer satisfaction approaches in process organizations are two steps behind those in product groups. Similarly, there is a maturity lag in *innovation execution* methodology. Most innovation methods for process improvement tend to be constructed around IT automation programs. The pitfall here is that many such projects are software package implementations, which are unlikely to be fast and iterative. The situation is different if the project involves new software to be programmed under Agile methodology; however, adopting completely new software is usually a smaller

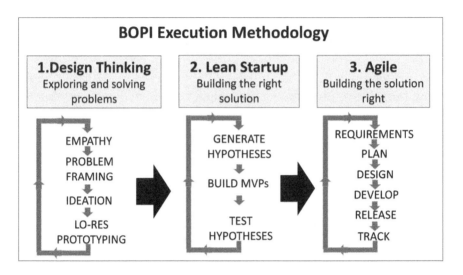

FIGURE 12: BOPI Execution Methodology

percentage of IT automation. That leaves us with the issue of fixing the maturity lag on process innovation methodology.

For fast and iterative process innovation, we find that combining Design Thinking, Lean Startup, and Agile methodology into one end-to-end innovation process works best (see Figure 12). These three methods are inherently complementary. When combined, they iteratively and rapidly deliver customer-oriented outcomes. The three methodologies are well-established in the industry, so this book will not cover them in depth.

At a high level, Design Thinking[35] simply helps us explore ideas sufficiently before we converge on a solution. It's an effective tool for addressing the real-world ambiguity associated with any design requirement, be it for a product or a process. It forces us to empathize with the customer, learn, frame the problem differently, and explore potential solutions.

Given a customer-centric problem statement, Lean Startup is then used to experiment with different options rapidly and iteratively. It helps us learn along the way while empowering people who are closest to the work to decide how best to achieve desired outcomes.[36]

Agile is all about doing projects in short "sprints," in which teams build a feature or a prototype, share it with the customer or stakeholder, then gather their feedback and revise it.[37] It allows project teams to adapt the plan more easily, identify flaws, and fix them sooner, as well as to look for better, cheaper, and faster ways to meet end user needs.

Together, these three methodologies take the risk out of developing suboptimal processes, because they enable us to avoid the waste of developing services that do not deliver the right business value. The point here is that being disciplined about using a business-value-obsessed methodology is critical in today's fast-changing world. Given the historically siloed origins of process organizations, in most places there isn't "one" process innovation method to begin with. And even if there is one, it often is not sufficiently business-value obsessed.

An Example of How Business-Value-Obsessed Process Innovation Works

The three BOPI action items—embracing customer discontent, connecting the dots, and fast and iterative innovation—are highly effective at maximizing process innovation value. They feed upon one another to create high-value and reliable process innovations, as we illustrate with the example of a new internal service created by P&G. The 2008 global economic crisis affected P&G as much as it did other companies. Cost reduction plans were therefore implemented, which impacted every business unit and every country. Among the cost cuts was a reduction in the travel and entertainment (T&E) budget. This was of course right to do, but at GBS we took the opportunity to ponder whether there might be even more business value opportunity in the T&E arena. We asked ourselves whether we could do more to maintain or grow collaboration across sites. And could that also be used to further reduce T&E spending?

The answer turned out to be a resounding yes. The process innovation was to introduce high-quality videoconference rooms that provided an experience as close as possible to meeting in person. Recall that this was in 2008, before Zoom or Teams existed. Video calls were unreliable at best and an unlikely contender against personal travel.

However, within nine months, 43 sites around the world (reflecting 80% of P&G's annual travel cost) had installed a service called Video Conference Solution (VCS). That further reduced the travel budget and created faster cycle times in operations, thanks to better cross-site collaboration. There were, of course, several problems that had to be solved along the way.

One major problem was that the videoconferencing technology at the time was not yet mature. And the company was not going to offer up an additional budget to innovate on this. Eventually, what GBS did was simple: it offered to further reduce its own travel and expenses budget for the year (over and above the corporate cost cut) and to reinvest the amount of that cut for the innovation. It also approached Cisco Systems, at that time the most mature partner for videoconferencing, to co-create a new gold standard video solution, which could then be commercialized by them to others.

The next challenge at the time was to make the process of connecting one room to another a single-click experience. Design Thinking was employed to tap into employees' needs. The solution was created iteratively and involved several failed experiments. However, in the end it did achieve the goal of having a one-click connection to any site in the world.

Meanwhile, to control the quality of the picture at any site in any country, the cameras, monitors, and even room layout were all chosen with a Steve Jobs–like obsession to details. Every piece of furniture in the VCS rooms, the color of the walls and carpets, the size and layout of the rooms—no detail was too small. The table in each room was semi-oval and faced as many as three large TV screens, which projected the exact same semi-oval table from the other connected site. The effect of the two semi-oval tables and similar room designs and colors made it seem as if the participants in the two sites were literally sitting across one oval table.

Similarly, Lean Startup and Agile methodology were used to implement the rooms iteratively so that execution was high-quality. All of this created a new video collaboration solution, which Cisco later made available to other companies. The new VCS product received numerous industry awards. Cisco's telepresence solution continued to gain market share in the aftermath. In hindsight though, perhaps the most important gain may have been that VCS laid the foundation for the next level of collaboration—virtual working across the company.

Checklist Items for Stage 3, *Open Market Rules*

To further strengthen your *Open Market Rules*, compare performance with the following Stage 3 characteristics:

- ☑ Process innovation delivers the complete potential of the customer value proposition—that is, beyond efficiency and effectiveness.

- ☑ Innovation is intentional. It is also measured through customer-aligned metrics so as to deliver increasing business value.

- ☑ Customer orientation goes well beyond satisfaction metrics. The user's needs as well as the client's are an obsession. They are the sources for generating new business value.

- ☑ Process innovations are diligent in connecting the dots among different possibilities to deliver even more potent business value.

- ☑ Process operations innovation is applied systemically, through consistent and broad-based application of frameworks (Design Thinking, Lean Startup, Agile).

10

Avoiding the Trap of Incremental Innovation in Processes

KEY INSIGHT: Incrementalism in process innovation is a significant issue. Fortunately, methodologies, organizing models, and trainings exist to overcome it.

In today's world, in which competitive advantage depends as much on process maturity as on product, the question is how to avoid lagging on process innovation. The reality in our experience is that for most organizations, process innovation isn't thought of as being on the same lofty plane as product innovation. There are understandable historical reasons for this. First, the siloed functional origins of business processes have long meant that process innovation has never been a big idea. Second, unlike in the product world, where product manager roles provide clear accountability for innovation, there hasn't been the equivalent service management construct until now. And finally, existing process ownership roles like GPO (global process owner) tend to prioritize standards-governance work rather than disruptive innovation. The result is that incrementalism in process innovation is a real pitfall. Meanwhile, digitally native organizations build both products and processes from a clean sheet of paper, placing traditional organizations at a serious disadvantage.

Once again, we can look for ideas by exploring the best innovation approaches in the product world. We will be deep-diving into the story of Samsung because it's a great organization that evolved from very traditional beginnings to the point that it is now recognized as among the most innovative companies in the world.

Samsung's Innovation Journey from Grocery to Electronics

The Boston Consulting Group (BCG) has published an innovation report each year since 2005 listing the top 50 innovative companies. The edition for 2021[38] includes all the usual suspects—Apple, Alphabet, Amazon, Alibaba, Fast Retailing, and Procter & Gamble. It also lists a company that was founded in 1938 as a trader in dried fish,[39] locally grown groceries, and noodles—Samsung. It ranks sixth on this list, which is not surprising, since it has been placed as high as #1[40] on Cap on Tap's catalog of the world's most innovative tech companies. How Samsung evolved from its humble beginnings in grocery into a conglomerate of about 80 companies ranging from clothing to shipping, telecoms, and, of course, electronics, is related partly to its innovation strategy. In the consumer electronics field, Samsung has had to crack the code on myriad topics, ranging from local to global, from closed innovation approaches to open, from layered decision-making to speedy decisions on innovation, and from situational innovation capability-building to systemic.

Samsung was founded as a grocery trading company by Lee Byung-Chul. After the Korean War it expanded into manufacturing and eventually into electronics. Founder Lee Byung-Chul was succeeded by his son Lee Kun-Hee in 1987. It was he who transformed the Samsung Electronics company into a global leader and an innovation powerhouse. Today Samsung Electronics is a consistent market leader and an innovation and design forerunner in all its product categories, which range from smartphones to LCD TVs to NAND flash memory. To achieve this, Samsung Electronics has had to excel in internal product innovation processes—identifying the right innovations, getting innovative products right, and getting the market execution right.

How Samsung Ensures the Right Innovations Get to Market

To win globally in consumer electronics, Samsung has had to excel at identifying the *few,* but *big,* product innovation ideas. Balancing diverse local market needs with big, global ideas is difficult, although not for the reasons one might expect. The issue can be less about local innovation ideas and more about innovation decision-making speed. Samsung worked through this issue in the early 1990s to speed up and globalize decision-making on innovation. In 1989, Samsung had between three and seven steps for project approval.[41] This consumed about 24 days for the seven layers of approval, including the final sign-off by the president. After the process was streamlined, by 1995 it took only three approvals, which could be obtained on the same day. Fast decision-making on big ideas has been a game-changer for the company. It was part of Samsung's early strategy for globalization, which involved streamlining decision-making and targeting international markets. Even the template for project proposals was in English, to foster globalized process management.

Samsung also had to work on an approach to separate the people who worked on transformational innovation from those who worked on the core business. For example, it recognized that in order to compete on the basis of innovative design, it would need people with new and different skills. So it moved its design center from a small town to Seoul in order to be closer to a valuable pool of young design professionals and industry experts.[42] Seperating the skills, people, and funding needed for *transformational* innovation from those needed for *continuous improvement* has worked well for them.

Samsung's Organizing Model for Product Innovation

Early in its life, Samsung Electronics understood the limitations of the closed innovation model, in which all skills are developed in-house. It had previously invested in the best people and centralized its R&D unit. That model struggles to keep up in the rapidly changing consumer world. Samsung changed its organizing model to open innovation, so that it could engage directly with customers and suppliers. Over time, it created a number of innovation initiatives and groups, most of which fell under Samsung Next. This was a multifaceted innovation group aimed at identifying new opportunities. It had several subgroups, including NEXT Product (in-house expert designers and engineers), Ventures (investing in startups), Mergers and Acquisitions (to acquire new companies), and Partnerships (for commercial collaboration opportunities with third parties). This open innovation model is not just an organizational construct for Samsung Electronics. It has penetrated Samsung's culture of innovation and is deeply embedded in Samsung's long-term strategy.[43]

Samsung's Approach to Building Innovation Capabilities

The third secret to success for Samsung Electronics has been its serious investment in training and development programs to help spread innovation capability throughout the organization. Besides providing internal training programs, it offers scholarships, postgraduate study opportunities, and international work placement for its staff in 120 offices across 57 countries.[44] As a byproduct, this links Samsung to renowned universities. Additionally, it has created new knowledge management tools and people rewards systems to enable strong knowledge discovery and sharing.

Lee Kun-Hee's quest for global leadership has enabled the company to deliver remarkable and systemic changes in how it innovates. The results? Samsung became the world's largest producer of memory chips in 1992, and LCD panels a decade later, and it continues to vie for global leadership in chipmaking. By 2012, Samsung Electronics had become the world's largest mobile phone maker by unit sales. It overtook Nokia and continues its global dominance, keeping ahead of current rivals like Apple and Xiaomi. By 2015, Samsung had more US patents approved than any other company, with more than 7,500 utility patents granted before the end of the year. It has become a recognized global brand, among the top five in Interbrand's ranking of the best brands.

Learning from Samsung on How to Innovate Big

For many reasons, the Samsung innovation story offers an excellent basis for lessons on accelerating process innovation. We like it because it suggests how to move from a traditional to a modernized approach for innovation. Samsung had to make deliberate changes in methodology, organizing model, and people capability to get there. Here are the most important lessons for process innovation.

Samsung developed a methodology to systemically identify the big ideas.

Samsung attacked the big-company problem of slow decision-making on innovation by reducing the number of layers in the approval process. They also ensured that disruptive innovation capacity was separated from core operations and organized those two differently. There are some great pointers for process organizations to take from this story. Let's first consider the approach to identifying big innovation ideas. Process innovations tend to be loaded in favor of the smaller ideas. In fact, most companies recognize this as a challenge. That is because traditional process organization goals are oriented toward cost reduction and stable service levels, both of which favor small fixes. To address this, companies turn to their program management office (PMO) to get more value via better prioritization of innovations. The PMO is a structure which provides expertise in professionally managing projects and optimizing portfolios. The way PMOs optimize the portfolio of initiatives is by stopping small ideas. This is not a good enough strategy. "Cutting the long tail" is an idea that suggests that stopping work on all small-value projects (i.e., the "tail") will free up capacity to work on the big idea projects. The problem is that there's a difference between stopping small ideas and developing new, big ones. Killing smaller ideas doesn't necessarily generate big ideas. PMO processes excel at resource assignment and optimization, not ideation. To be clear, PMOs offer important operational disciplines. But let's not confuse them with delivering new, big, breakthrough ideas—especially when it comes to process innovations. We need different approaches to generate big ideas for process innovation. We will address this later as part of our recommended model for big process innovation.

Samsung has an organizing model for big innovations.

When Samsung switched from relying solely on internal closed innovation to open innovation, it created an organizing model to generate more big ideas. The open innovation approach is now widespread in product organizations across industries. When combined with *Unified Accountability* via product managers, which ensures that products stay competitive, this works very effectively. In the process innovation world, two issues hamper this. One is the fact that *Unified Accountability*–based roles, such as service managers, are new and therefore accountability for innovation is still occasionally fuzzy. Another is that open approaches to process innovation are rare. Again, we will address this when we get to the big idea innovation model in this chapter.

Samsung is highly invested in systemic organization capability building for innovation.

The Samsung story illustrates how systematic capability building is used. It includes training, broadening assignments, university partnerships, and external vendor partnerships, all of which help drive innovation skills as well as mindsets deeper into the organization. In most process organizations, even when there is some innovation capability building, it is usually related to running operations rather than to innovation. The reality is that we need both. Therefore, our model for Stage 3 *Unified Accountability* incorporates this and other needs (see below).

The Model: Big Value Creation from Process Innovation

Avoiding incrementalism in process innovation requires a few deliberate decisions. As you may have gathered from the lessons highlighted via the Samsung story, these choices are related to innovation methodology, organizing model, and systemic organization capability-building.

Have a methodology that separates disruptive process innovation from continuous improvement and daily operations.

Big process innovations will come systematically if there is a disciplined innovation process for identifying disruptive process ideas. The fact is that most companies don't even have a business process innovation organization, let alone *disruptive* process innovation teams. That's another lesson we need to learn from "running processes as if they were a product business." For ongoing competitive advantage from business operations, we need dedicated effort on business process innovation.

Furthermore, we need a balanced portfolio of process innovation. A good mix of process innovation ideas should include (a) ideas that improve daily operations, (b) those that enable continuous evolution of processes, and (c) game-changing disruptive process ideas—called 10X ideas—for delivering 10-times-the-impact as opposed to just 10% improvements. Examples of how companies mix innovation across these types of ideas abound: Google (now Alphabet) has long championed the 70-20-10 model. That's essentially a 70-20-10 ratio of employee capacity for innovation.

Specifically,

- 70% of people's capacity is dedicated to operating the core business

- 20% of their capacity is related to continuous improvements to the core business

- 10% of their capacity is spent on disruptive new businesses

In a *Harvard Business Review* article, Bansi Nagji and Geoff Tuff[45] noted that companies that allocated 70% of their innovation activity to core initiatives, 20% to adjacent ones, and 10% to transformational ones outperformed their peers by a P/E premium of between 10% and 20%. This is equally relevant for the process innovation mix. To be clear, the 70-20-10 ratio isn't a universal formula. Your industry or organization may be just fine with 80-19-1, or 90-8-2, or whatever. What is important is being deliberate in planning for big disruptive opportunities in process innovation, separate from adjacent or core ones.

Adopt an open organizing model along with clear accountability.

There are two parts to this. The first relates to the use of an open innovation model. That term refers to collaboration among companies, individuals, and external agencies to deliver innovation while sharing risks and rewards. This model has been a proven success in process innovation as well. Open innovation seems logical in this arena, especially for big ideas. Technology providers would prefer to innovate with real client companies and actual users. The clients benefit from early access to innovative products at lower risk and cost. They don't need to own the intellectual property of the innovation to benefit from its use.

The second part to this is *Unified Accountability* for delivering the outcomes. Open innovation models can be risky unless clear accountability for results is assigned. That accountability is best assigned to service managers, who are the equivalent of product managers in the process management context.

Build systemic innovation capability via skills, talent, and rewards.

Process organizations usually have a strong background in analytical and operational skills. That is often reinforced with reward systems to improve process reliability and reduce costs. For holistic process improvement, we must complement this with innovation capability building—we need additional talent, skills, and rewards. Practices for identifying and grooming innovation talent need to be put in place. Additional capability development in both left-brained and right-brained skills must be implemented. But perhaps most importantly, there must be reward systems in place to create a receptive atmosphere in the organization for new ideas. Creating reward systems and a culture that encourages big thinking always pays off. There are many program ideas out there for "intrapreneurship" (i.e., approaches to developing entrepreneurship mindsets inside the company). One well-known example is Google's (Alphabet's) renowned management philosophy of the "20 percent time." The idea is simple: encourage every employee to work on whatever they think will most benefit Google, on top of their regular workload. Famous 20% projects include products like Google News, Gmail, and AdSense. The push for 20% time may have waxed and waned over the years, but the *idea* of that 20% is important. Talented and creative people can be given a framework to work on big ideas outside of formal oversight.

Deliberate and disciplined strategies to drive bigger process innovations are a must in a world in which there is as much competitive advantage to be had from processes as from products. The key is to begin with clear accountability for big process innovation outcomes and then build methodologies, organizing models, and people capability around them.

Checklist Items for Stage 3, *Unified Accountability*

To strengthen *Unified Accountability*, compare performance with the following Stage 3 characteristics:

- ☑ Accountability for innovation in process operations is clear and exercised effectively. It plays out at all levels in the organization, for the respective services.

- ☑ Proliferation of small, "long tail" ideas that create distraction and don't add much value is well recognized and addressed.

- ☑ A methodology is in place to identify big ideas. A balanced mix of continuous operations improvement and disruptive new initiatives is in place.

- ☑ There is an organizing model in place based on open innovation, along with clear accountability for innovation results via a service management role.

- ☑ Deliberate talent management, skill development, and reward systems are implemented for process innovation to generate new business value.

11

Mastering Business-Centricity for Processes Innovation

KEY INSIGHT: Going from a transactional to a business-centric relationship with internal client organizations is a critical step for maximizing business value.

As we round out the Stage 3 maturity of process operations, let's start with a key question—what's the best relationship we could possibly set up between a process organization and its business unit clients? For inspiration, we can look to what the best vendors, including consulting organizations, do. They view going from a transactional relationship to a strategic partnership as a critical goal. The best partners don't want to be strategic in name alone. They seek to be as invested in the success of their client company as any employee of the client. They strive to be embedded in the client's world, not so that they can sell more, but so that they can deliver the best win–win business value. They do that through better operational quality and better innovation ideas. Top-notch client managers do this intuitively. Professional consulting companies like the Big Four have fine-tuned this approach to a science over the years.

The equivalent of the Big Four consulting vendors inside the company can be the internal process organization. However, in our experience, most internal process organizations are in the early stages of maturity in professionalizing business unit client management. There are great insights to be gained regarding how the best strategic partnerships have been achieved between suppliers and clients in the external world. We examine the story of how P&G evolved from a transactional to a client-centric relationship with Walmart.

P&G and Walmart Set Up a Win-Win Relationship

When Walmart founder and CEO Sam Walton ran into Procter & Gamble CEO John Smale in the mid-1980s, he had what might be one of the more interesting "good news/bad news" conversations in business history. He mentioned that P&G had been chosen for the prestigious Vendor of the Year award! And the bad news?…He had decided to give it to another supplier.

Here's what had happened. Walton had tried calling Smale with the good news that P&G would be awarded the honor. P&G was already a major supplier at the time, doing $350Mn[46] in business with Walmart. Unfortunately, the sales organization had given Walton a P&G corporate phone number to call Smale. After being transferred five or six times, Walton hung up. The problem was not just the inability to connect to Smale. This incident reflected the impersonal relationship between the two companies.

Fortunately, Smale took the hint, and soon after, he assigned three full-time senior leaders to the Walmart headquarters to ensure better collaboration. That was the start of, as they say, "a beautiful relationship" between the two companies. What eventually came out of that incident would serve as a model for customer-focused relationships, which would transform the way the consumer package industry and others organized themselves for channel partnerships. Other companies would follow over time, setting up a small city of more than 1,000 "Walmart customer teams" in northwestern Arkansas.

P&G grew its Walmart sales from $350Mn in 1987 to $13Bn in 2013.[47] This partnership linked sales, supply chain, accounting, and several other processes across the two companies. For instance, P&G was electronically connected into Walmart's data systems, so it effectively knew when every individual product left Walmart stores. It was able to ship replenishments to Walmart's distribution centers perfectly timed to go dock-to-dock, from P&G's trucks to Walmart's trucks going out to stores.

"If I want to punish any of my buyers, I put them on P&G's business."

In 1988, the relationship between P&G and Walmart was transactional. The two companies had similar relationship styles[48] and were powerful traditional organizations that negotiated hard. To be sure, their business performances were interdependent: they needed each other to be successful. But in a hard-charging transactional relationship, negotiation power trumped longer-term win–win strategies. On-the-ground relationships were strained to the point that Sam Walton declared that if he wanted to punish any of his buyers, he put them on P&G's business. Despite the friction, both companies were growing their shared businesses nicely. P&G's Walmart business was around $350Mn; however, the market share of its products at Walmart was lower than in the national market. This presented an opportunity for the two companies to build a stronger relationship.

The Industry Model for Key Account Management

To develop the new Walmart customer team design, several interventions were made. First, P&G set up additional dedicated resources at Walmart's headquarters in Arkansas. It eliminated elaborate legal contracts from their relationship and replaced them with letters of intent. The two companies set up a joint vision and goals and assigned multifunctional resource people, who would work directly with their counterparts in the other company to achieve those goals. The customer/supplier interaction changed from a "bow tie" type design, where the two companies met only at the middle of the bow tie via the sales organization, to an "inverted bow tie" or diamond-like structure

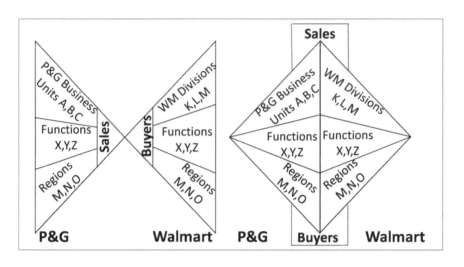

FIGURE 13: Bow Tie vs. Diamond Engagement Models

(see Figure 13), where the two companies had broad touch points with counterparts, at multiple levels and in multiple functions. Perhaps most importantly, they agreed to openly share business data across the two companies.

As a result of all these changes, business and profitability grew significantly for both companies. This in turn set up a new model for customers and retailers to partner across the whole industry. Today, most large retailers and their big suppliers have some form of organizing model where a diamond structure encourages direct interactions between multifunctional data and people. Client-focused structures like these change the relationships from transactional to business-centric. Transactional customer/supplier relationships negotiate on a win–lose basis; it's about who should enjoy the larger piece of the pie. Business-centric relationships encourage collaboration to grow the size of the total pie. That's true of customer/supplier relationships *external* to the company, and it's also true of client/supplier relationships *within* the company (i.e., process organization relationships with business customers).

Learning from the P&G–Walmart Key Account Management Story

The P&G–Walmart story is useful because it elegantly serves up the answer to many issues that process organizations have regarding internal business unit clients. For instance, how do we streamline the many-to-many relationships between processes and clients? That requires solving a Rubik's cube of many dimensions, including multiple processes (finance, HR, IT, supply chain, etc.), multiple business units, multiple functional officers, and multiple geographic business leaders. Another challenge is how to balance between the conflicting needs of standardizing for scale and personalizing for agility. That requires a mindset change. To paraphrase Sam Walton, "If the business process organizations thought of themselves as an extension of a given business unit, would they treat it differently?"

Once again, we don't need to reinvent the wheel when creating an operating engine for client management. We can learn from the P&G–Walmart key account management structure. Yes, there are some differences (e.g., the client in the case of a process organization is inside the company), but the same principles still apply. Next, we flesh out the key parts of the business process client management model.

The Model: Business Process Client Management

Client management for business processes is similar to the original P&G-Walmart context with two differences. First, in the case of Walmart, there was originally a single-point relationship between the Walmart buyer and the P&G sales representative, within the bow tie structure. But in the case of business processes, the internal/client needs several business processes in order to run the business (supply chain, HR, etc.). That's a one-to-many relationship. Second, the client is senior enough that they don't use many of the process offerings themselves (e.g., processing a sales order). That means there is no personal relationship. Thus, as Figure 14 illustrates, we start with an imperfect

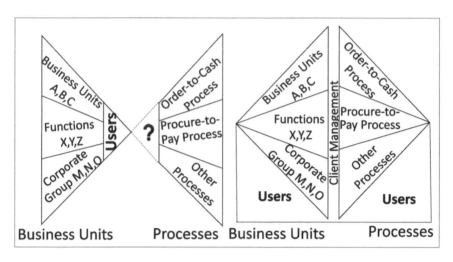

FIGURE 14: Transactional vs. Business-Centric Engagement Models

bow tie. The good news is that the recommended "diamond" model still applies. This, however, requires a cross-process client manager to be assigned to each client. It also requires the client manager to be embedded in the leadership team of the client. Let's illustrate how this might work with a hypothetical situation. Let's take a global company with regional business units. The regions have profit-and-loss responsibilities. Now let's focus on one client—for example, the Middle East and Africa (MEA) region. The president of MEA has valid concerns about various business processes ranging from payroll to logistics, which are pushing global standards and vendors. In a region like MEA, these result in expensive, slow, and unsuitable process solutions.

In our client management model for business processes, we would reapply the P&G–Walmart customer team approach. What if there was a dedicated senior person within the MEA regional unit who reported to the leader of the MEA unit as well as to the global process organization. And what if their job was to make sure that both day-to-day operations and ongoing personalized innovations were delivered for MEA? If we think about this role just for a minute, this is not dissimilar to the structure of a traditional "account manager" for a critical supplier.

There are some important differences in the sense that this account manager works for the same company, and we will get to the implications of that later. For now, assume that we create such a role—"client manager"—for operational processes for the MEA business.

How does such a role work? The core of this idea reflects the same principle of common vision and goals, as mentioned in the P&G–Walmart story. At the start of year, there would be agreement on a common set of goals, plans, and targets specific to the MEA unit. These would include operational goals, such as cost, service levels, and so on, as well as transformational goals such as projects to deliver continuous improvement to specific business processes in MEA, as well as disruptive goals, such as innovations that will dramatically change the landscape of one or two processes in MEA. This could be called the "Joint Business Plan" (JBP), which is incidentally what the customer and retailer organizations do too. During the year, as the work is executed, progress is reported, and ongoing changes are made as necessary to the JBP to ensure that it delivers maximum value to MEA. Over the past two decades, this client management model has been shown to maximize innovation and business value. It does require some nuances in design, which we will elaborate below via the same MEA example.

1. **The client manager must be a senior person** who is empowered to get results within both the MEA team and the global process teams. This is one of the benefits of having the client manager working within the same company. This person could report to the MEA business leader as well as to the process organization. They could be a part of ongoing leadership discussions of business strategy and business plans for the MEA region. A good client manager would then take steps to tweak global operations and processes to support these plans.

2. **The client manager must represent all operational processes.** The problem with having a different client manager for every process (e.g., one each for source-to-pay (S2P), accounting

record-to-report, order-to-cash, and so on) in one MEA business unit team is in the complexity of that structure. It's not just suboptimal; it actually reinforces process silos. The answer is to have one client manager in charge of all operational processes. That person would then work with the respective business process owners to ensure that the best value is delivered to MEA. This is where the "inverse bow tie" comes into play.

Once again, this is not dissimilar to having an account manager from say, a Big Four consulting firm who works back within their organization to pull together the best value from multiple internal vertical teams. The other benefit of a client manager is that they provide single-point accountability across all processes, which is often missing.

In Closing

The client management model for business processes is sophisticated. It delivers high business value at higher levels of process maturity in a company. Also, because it is so sophisticated, it must be applied in specific situations and with certain prerequisites. One important prerequisite is that we assume the existence of some type of a global operations organization (GOO) or a Global Business Services (GBS) structure. The client manager needs to represent all business process delivery to the business unit. That makes a lot of sense if we think about this in the context of a Stage 3 maturity level. In previous chapters, we progressed from siloed business processes to E2E ones. We also introduced standard methods for ensuring transparency of operations, such as transparency in the pricing of services. Those things lead to the formation of a common, centralized operation for business processes. Whether this is a GBS structure, or a desiloed structure under a chief operations officer (COO), or something else is immaterial; it is important at this juncture that a seamless organization exist for operations across finance, marketing, sales, IT, supply chain, and so forth.

As mentioned earlier, this client management model has been tested out and is acknowledged to be the best operating engine for customer-centric operations. When folded together with the two other design elements from the previous two chapters (i.e., business value obsession and big ideas), we now have a systemic approach to innovation in business processes. Stage 3 process organizations deliver efficiency, effectiveness, and innovation. In the final trio of chapters for Stage 4, we will further raise the bar to target outright process leadership.

Checklist Items for Stage 3, *Dynamic Operating Engine*

To strengthen the *Dynamic Operating Engine*, compare performance with the following Stage 3 characteristics:

- ☑ "False positives" in business value are preempted. These include new technologies for technology's sake as well as flavor-of-the-month tools.

- ☑ Business operations "client managers" are embedded in the business's leadership teams. This enables constant focus and rapid response to issues and opportunities.

- ☑ Interaction between the business and the operations organization is enabled at all points of contact. The liaison with internal business partners is, as for external customers, based on continuous value creation and innovation.

- ☑ The operations organization is designed to constantly detect needed changes and swiftly respond to them.

- ☑ Clear metrics and measures are in place and are totally aligned, documented, and regularly validated. There is absolutely no confusion with regard to value creation, and when there is, adjustments are made immediately.

PART V

Stage 4 of Business Processes— *Responsive Maturity*

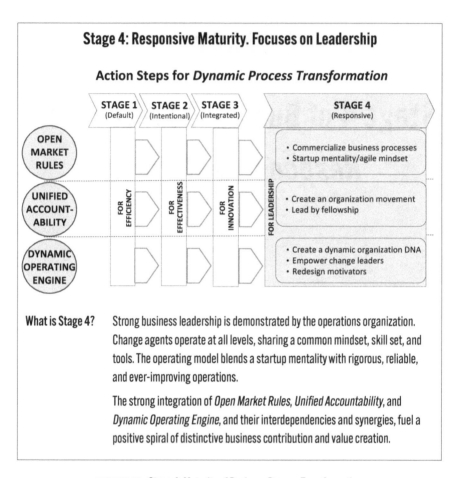

Stage 4: Responsive Maturity. Focuses on Leadership

Action Steps for *Dynamic Process Transformation*

What is Stage 4? Strong business leadership is demonstrated by the operations organization. Change agents operate at all levels, sharing a common mindset, skill set, and tools. The operating model blends a startup mentality with rigorous, reliable, and ever-improving operations.

The strong integration of *Open Market Rules*, *Unified Accountability*, and *Dynamic Operating Engine*, and their interdependencies and synergies, fuel a positive spiral of distinctive business contribution and value creation.

FIGURE 15: Stage 4, Maturity of Business Process Transformation

12

How to Commercialize
Business Processes

> **KEY INSIGHT:** It is possible to extract even more value from efficient, effective, and innovative business processes. We need to reapply the approaches used by companies to commercialize their products.

If you're thinking to yourself, "Wait! Commercialize business processes? This doesn't apply to me because we have no intention of selling our operations externally," then hold on. That's not it. We're talking about something else that is extremely relevant to all business process organizations.

Here's the thing—if we are ever going to have business processes become a competitive advantage for our company, then we're going to need supplementary leadership skills. We are referring in particular to thought leadership for processes and, of course, to turning that thought leadership into sustained business value. That requires further skills, such as managing by influence. Stage 4 maturity is all about going beyond process efficiency, effectiveness, and innovation to embrace this type of leadership. That means reinforcing right-brain skills like communicating, relationship building, and adapting.

One way of thinking about the trio of chapters in Stage 4 is that they deal with balancing left-brain and right-brain skills. The capabilities needed for business process transformation at earlier maturity levels were more weighted toward *management* skills, whereas higher maturity requires more *leadership*. What these additional skills look like, and how to go about utilizing them, is the focus of this section, starting with commercialization capabilities.

In earlier chapters we talked about how to run business processes as if they were products. By the end of Stage 3 maturity, we have developed all the elements of "product mindset" execution. At Stage 4, we must proceed to the next step, which we might expect from any entrepreneur who has created a great product—successful commercialization to unlock its full impact. Let's continue to draw lessons from the product world as we explore how commercialization skills can lift our business processes to sustained value creation. This time we delve into the global company that created WeChat—Tencent.

How Tencent Commercialized as a Startup

It's hard to converse about social media these days without the "m" word being thrown at you within minutes. We're talking about the "metaverse." And Tencent is a company that created a metaverse before today's metaverse. But let's back up a bit to define this word. Simply put, the metaverse is "a virtual-reality space in which users can interact with a computer-generated environment, and other users."[49] The problem is that most experts don't define the word simply. So *Verge* magazine, in an article intended to simplify the hype, informs us that "the Metaverse is an expansive network of persistent, real-time rendered 3D worlds and simulations that support continuity of identity, objects, history, payments, and entitlements, and can be experienced synchronously by an effectively unlimited number of users, each with an individual sense of presence."[50] Simple! Any questions?

But we digress....

Long before today's metaverse existed, before Facebook or Twitter or WeChat were even born, Tencent launched a virtual reality space for social media users. It was called QQ Show, and it launched in January 2003. Which is why QQ Show is sometimes called the metaverse 1.0.

Its successful commercialization is what made Tencent a viable company. Before that, it was just another startup with a good product without financial viability. In other words, without the commercialization of QQ Show, Tencent and all its current products—WeChat, TenPay, QQ Wallet, Qzone, Tencent Games—might not exist today. Some of these products may be unfamiliar to Western users, but they are huge in the rest of the world. And the story of Tencent's launch and successful commercialization carries deep lessons for dynamic business process transformation.

Tencent Commercializes QQ Show, and the Rest Is History

In 2002, Tencent's core product, QQ, had hundreds of millions of users but no viable future. QQ was a free instant messaging service. Unless Tencent could translate that traffic into revenue, the company would die. Tencent's solution was to develop and commercialize a variation on its product called QQ Show. This built further on instant messaging by allowing users to create avatars. In this virtual world, users could try out cute images or fashions on their avatar pictures, inspired by the Korean Wave at the time. They could also use a virtual currency named Q Coin to buy designs. This may be starting to sound similar to today's metaverse world. We now see why QQ Show is called Metaverse 1.0. QQ Show was launched in January 2003. Within six months, it had 5 million paid users. Finally, Tencent had a viable future!

After that, Tencent kept launching hit after hit. In 2005, there was Qzone—a multimedia social networking service. Then came the megasuccessful WeChat in 2011, followed by additional capabilities like WeChat Pay, a game center, entertainment services like Tencent Video and QQ Music, a Cloud platform, and many others. Today, WeChat is synonymous with modern day-to-day social media in China. Tencent went on to become one of the world's ten most valuable companies in April 2017. By 2022, it was the only Chinese company on that list, ranking 10th in the world (incidentally, Meta ranked 11th). For Tencent it was a far cry from the days of being turned down by investors. The tipping point was its successful commercialization in 2003.

Tencent's Typical Challenge as an Early Dotcom Startup

Tencent's story goes back to the Wild West days of the internet. Tales of hitting it big were everywhere, including of course in China. In this landscape, Ma Huateng (better known as Pony Ma) hit upon a unique idea. Could we use the internet for email, news, and other applications via personal handheld devices?

Over time, Tencent reorganized into two separate businesses—wireless paging and a free instant messaging service for PCs called OICQ. The latter exploded in popularity in China. By the end of 1999, OICQ had a million users. But Tencent continued to lose money, not unlike many other dotcom startups. To address this, Tencent put itself up for sale. When it found no takers, it sought venture capital funding. Soon after, two rounds of capital infusion allowed Tencent to evolve its product (now relaunched as QQ) and to scale its operations further. However, in 2002, monetization of its instant messaging business for sustained revenue continued to be elusive. Earlier, even though it had a base of an astonishing 100 million users, Yahoo had declined to buy it out.

Ma's only other option was to commercialize Tencent.

But What Exactly Is Commercialization?

It is time we defined "commercialization." Terms like marketing, communications, and commercialization are often treated as if they were interchangeable. The term at hand had long been associated with entrepreneurship. With the rise of the tech industry, and its consequent need to commercialize its products and technologies, the term became popular with a somewhat different meaning than before.

In essence, in the product world, *to commercialize* is to *go to market in a profitable and scaled manner*. Companies need to commercialize in order to make their products or services viable. It is in that sense that commercialization differs from monetization (charging for your product), or marketing (understanding the needs of consumers or customers and communicating to them). So yes, commercialization does include activities for productization, marketing, and communication. But it uses all of these to generate the broader outcome of delivering an ongoing viable business model operating at profit and at scale.[51]

Tencent's QQ Show launch was a successful commercialization because it turned traffic into revenue, at a profit, and systemically. This ensured that Tencent would be able to scale. Which brings us back to a key question—is commercialization relevant only to products as opposed to business processes? In fact, it can be applied to processes too. In the context of business processes, commercialization is the good old synergy formula of two plus two equals five. It's powerful because it takes pieces of existing business process solutions and finds new ways to extract value from them. Commercialization is thus a higher-level systemic "platform" for viably leveraging any product or process capability. By platform, we mean a multidisciplinary effort that includes communications, marketing, and productization, to keep the business value growing viably. Which is why commercialization is a perfect model for taking good Stage 3 business processes and turning them into ongoing, viable, Stage 4 competitive advantage.

The Key Learning: Commercialize for Ongoing Viability

Successful commercialization tips the scale in the product world from having good product capability to having an ongoing viable business model.

Let's examine what it takes to commercialize products in companies like Tencent.

1. **Develop a mindset of winning in the open market:** First, there is a huge *mindset* difference between successful productization and commercialization. Pony Ma was relentless in evolving Tencent's business model to complement changes to his product. Entrepreneurs like him are constantly evolving their products in search of successful commercialization. These product evolutions are driven by a mindset of doing whatever it takes to

win in the marketplace. Tencent evolved from pagers to instant messaging, OICQ, Qcoin, and QQ Show in rapid succession. That's a remarkable pace of evolution for any business model. Each step was market driven.

2. **Focus relentlessly on the user:** User experience was, and continues to be, a bigger priority for Tencent and WeChat than for, say, Facebook or Twitter. For instance, WeChat at one time limited the number of native ads shown in a user's WeChat Moments feed (photo sharing app) to one per day. This was to balance its monetization priorities with user experience.

3. **Deliver against investor expectations:** A focus on returns to investors is common in the startup world. It was also a factor in the successful commercialization of Tencent. Both rounds of capital infusion delivered significant returns to the funders. Viable commercialization of QQ Show then turbocharged those returns.

4. **Create adjacent products:** Tencent was very successful in launching adjacent apps that kept building on the QQ platform and later on WeChat. In fact, Tencent has been much more aggressive than any of its Western counterparts when it comes to adding features, which range from mobile wallet to placing online orders, tracking deliveries, paying bills, and comparing prices.

These four capabilities—an open-market mindset, win the user, win the client (investor), and drive adjacencies—are core lessons for our model for commercializing business processes.

The Model: Commercialize Business Processes

Before we apply these four capabilities to business processes, let's put our *Dynamic Process Transformation* journey into context. So far, our work processes have delivered *efficiencies* at Stage 1 and *effectiveness* at

Stage 2 and have become *innovative* at Stage 3. Now at Stage 4, the business process organization is starting to exercise thought leadership to become the *sustained operational transformation engine* for the enterprise. The model for process commercialization will help do that. We can use the lessons from Tencent here.

1. Open Market Mindset

In the first three stages of *Dynamic Process Transformation*, most mature business process leaders will have benchmarked their operations against those of peer companies. So, for example, how does the performance of our sales organization, in terms of productivity, ability to grow the top line, and preferred supplier status, compare with that of peer companies? That's a good start, but it's not enough to avoid an incoming disruption. For instance, it is entirely possible that a digitally native company is innovating on an online distribution channel, which could make our traditional sales model obsolete. In this regard, an open market mindset will instill the following:

a. **Questioning of the status quo:** Just because a process is fine now doesn't mean it will be the best option in the future.

b. **Taking personal accountability:** It will empower people to take educated risks on business process evolution.

c. **Development of contextual intelligence:** It will ensure that process standards and expertise will be used only in the appropriate context.

We can develop these by being deliberate and disciplined in training process leaders in these skills. Most process excellence development programs miss these capabilities.

2. Win the User

Much of the existing literature on process management has focused on user experience (UX). However, we need to go much further in Stage 4. There are aspects of leadership skills related to anticipating user needs, to delivering compelling communications, and to creating long-lasting adoption, that are a full step beyond UX. Hence the term "*winning* the user." Let's illustrate with a common challenge in most organizations—IT systems implementation. According to the eLearning industry,[52] about 75% of all systems implementation projects fail due to user adoption issues. Despite the significant emphasis on UX in the past decade, this percentage has not changed enough.

Here's the issue. We need to think about systems or process implementations as habit changes. That involves three steps. First, create or find the right solution to the problem. Second, create a fertile ground and reward system for using the solution. Third, foster the personal motivation to try it out. UX is very effective on the first but not as much on the second and third. If we might be forgiven for tinkering with the adage that "you can lead a horse to water, but you can't make it drink," then the first step creates the perfect pool of water, the second leads the horse to the pool, and the third makes it drink. We need three different approaches to these issues. UX for the first, adoption methodologies for the second, and professional communications for the third.

Once again, this calls for new competency development for process leaders. This disciplined capability is currently not fully developed.

3. Win the Customer

To go from process excellence to process commercialization, we need to *win* the customer. Recall that the equivalent of *customers* in the internal business process world are the heads of the business units or functions that bear the costs of the process operations (closing books, running facilities, offering workplaces, etc.). These are the "line" leaders, who are proxy customers for business value creation. By Stage 3 of process maturity we've already implemented strategic alignment programs (as mentioned in the previous chapter) via customer team structures and annual joint business planning. So, what's missing?

The problem has to do with the chasm between the clients (senior executive stakeholders) and the day-to-day operations folks in the process organizations. There's a vast difference between customer awareness and customer *intimacy*. In the external product world, legions of highly compensated market researchers track and shadow every action of customers. They do this not because they don't know what customers "want" but because they want to be intimate with customer "needs"—*possibly getting to those that were never expressed.*

To commercialize our business processes, we need to ensure that the business operations people have the opportunity for *intimacy*. If our business process transactions are mostly operated by teams located at a remote site, be it physical or virtual, and if there are neither opportunities nor rewards for customer intimacy, then what we'll likely get is "customer alignment" rather than "being one with the customer." We can address that by providing (a) disciplined competency development, (b) the opportunity for customer intimacy via job rotation, and (c) updated reward systems for the operations organization.

4. Drive Adjacencies

We mentioned earlier how Tencent kept developing adjacent products to WeChat, such as mobile wallet, online ordering, tracking deliveries, paying bills, and price comparison. That increased the value of their product to customers. That's another commercialization lesson to bring to process management. We can be more deliberate in building value-adds in adjacent areas of the business process. Let's illustrate this with the very common business process of record-to-report (R2R).

The financial recording and reporting processes of most organizations entail a predictable series of steps. First, capture all financial transactions for either revenue (e.g., sales) or cost (e.g., purchases) in the financial books. Next, commence data sharing across different fiscal entities in the company. Then initiate general ledger closing. After that, consolidate financial data across all units of the business. And, finally, run all reporting needs (internal financial reports, external-to-company reporting, and regulatory reporting). Most companies do have all of this streamlined and automated. However, what they are potentially missing is the adjacent value to the R2R process. For instance, how about using AI to harness the power of the myriad Excel sheets—which hundreds of users employ at the input or output sides of R2R—for better financial forecasting? Or the tremendous power of prescriptive advanced analytics to automate some decision-making regarding sales or expenses for each major decision-maker? There are large pools of value at the intersections of business processes. We can tap these adjacent benefits.

These four capabilities of business process commercialization—open market mindset, win the user, win the customer (stakeholder), and drive adjacencies—are the secret to creating ongoing, viable new business value. Process commercialization brings the mindset of two plus two equals five to unearth previously untapped value. We share how by turning to a *Harvard Business Review* success story titled "How P&G Presents Data to Decision-Makers."[53]

An Example of Commercialization: P&G's Business Sphere

By 2009, most of P&G's business processes, such as finance, HR, IT, and supply chain, had been centralized and substantially automated. Decision support services, whether via standard report formats or visual dashboards and analytics, were provided as centralized services. Meanwhile, P&G's Global Business Services (GBS) organization also ran physical building facilities, as well as IT infrastructure services like audioconferencing and other meeting services. The question was, could we take all these mature Stage 3 services and create further value at their intersections? And could we commercialize them to create a hitherto unknown *ongoing, viable,* and *leveraged* "use case"? This turned out to be a new GBS service called Business Sphere, which was the subject of the aforementioned *HBR* article.

In this case, commercialization meant creating a new adjacent idea: enabling faster and better senior leaders' decision-making. P&G's global business leadership team met every Monday to review the company's performance. In the era before Zoom or Teams, this was done via audioconferencing and pre-reading of standard reports distributed via email. The new Stage 4 process transformation idea was to improve decision-making via three ingredients:

1. Redesign the boardrooms at the P&G HQ, and at all participating regional and business unit headquarters, to make participants feel closer to each other even when they were geographically dispersed. This meant adding dedicated, high-quality videoconferencing between chosen meeting rooms, along with high-quality motion-picture screen displays so that participants could see the same business data together. (Again, remember that this was before mass videoconferencing and other meeting technologies.)

2. Create a data visualization and analytics platform to present the specific data needed for the company's Monday morning decision meetings. This eliminated discussions around "your data accuracy versus mine." It was *one version of the truth*, which could be drilled down and analyzed in real-time.

3. Add dedicated analyst support for the leadership meetings. In preparing for these meetings, the CEO and his team members could call upon an expert, who in today's world would be called a data scientist. The leaders could get the best data and analysis possible *before* the meeting so that the meeting itself could focus on decision-making.

But the new Business Sphere wasn't just a collection of the above three items. It was a higher-order "platform" for ongoing innovation, on which more and more adjacent "use cases" would be built over the years, ranging from specialized decision support, such as the new planograms of product shelves with a given retailer, to inventory management and virtual supply chain simulations.

The learning from this case study is that the highest level of business process excellence does not end with integrating processes end-to-end. It doesn't even end after creating a new solution for better and faster decision-making. Bringing together building blocks of different process capabilities and finding new ways to extract even more business value via commercialization is an endless source of possibilities.

Checklist Items for Stage 4, *Open Market Rules*

To further strengthen your *Open Market Rules*, compare performance with the following Stage 4 characteristics:

- ☑ Business operations are run with a mindset of "winning in the open market," as opposed to internal "back office" or commodity.

- ☑ There is relentless focus on the user, the stakeholder, and the customer. This is not just declared or a good intention, but measurable and measured.

- ☑ Processes are commercialized like business products: additional and ongoing value is unlocked constantly.

- ☑ The status quo is constructively challenged in order to find ever new ways to bring distinctive value to the business.

- ☑ Leadership is demonstrated visibly at all levels. Effective, innovative solutions are cross-pollinated to adjacent areas to amplify the value creation. This is deliberate, planned, and based on customer input.

13

How to Create a Movement for Sustained Process Transformation

> KEY INSIGHT: The fastest way to change a company culture is to create a movement. This requires leadership ability to manage by fellowship and to anticipate business needs proactively.

To understand why it is important to create a movement to change a company culture, let's back up a bit. When we think of creating perpetual business process excellence, we're essentially talking about a systemic culture change. The difference between a one-off process transformation and sustained competitive advantage lies in creating the ongoing mindset of constant pursuit of excellence. We know that this is extremely difficult and that culture change projects often fail. However, the main reason they fail is eye-opening. Based on research done by the NeuroLeadership Institute,[54] the biggest factor in failure is not lack of investment or insufficient support, or lack of top management commitment or focus. No, the biggest factor is failure to change human habits. We all have experienced that. But this merely shifts our question: how do we go about changing human habits in large numbers? And that's where starting a movement comes in.

The creation of a movement is more typically associated with social, religious, or political transformation. Furthermore, it's often linked to big, wicked-dilemma-type changes. Mahatma Gandhi, Mother Teresa,

Dr. Martin Luther King, and, more recently, Greta Thunberg have created inspirational movements that are bigger than themselves. These have lasted, or will last, well beyond their lifetimes. But is it reasonable to expect dramatic movements to come from the average person like you or me? Can the concept of a movement be extended to corporate culture change?

We intuitively know that in the case of process transformation, this is possible. We also know that the biggest challenge is to change habits. We further know that process changes are inconvenient and cause organizational inertia. And we know that very often executives don't directly control all the resources. These are not unsurmountable challenges. We know of successful examples of movements in other contexts, and these can be used for process transformation too. We call this approach "managing by fellowship." Let's illustrate this with an example.

The Gillette Acquisition Story: Finding the Best Time to Change Processes

There is never a convenient time to introduce process change in an organization. At Procter & Gamble, we were faced with this dilemma during the acquisition and subsequent integration of the Gillette company into P&G. More specifically, about a year into the integration of business processes, people, and systems from Gillette, a substantial challenge arose that was specific to the Braun business unit, which was one of the three main divisions in the Gillette company. If we continued to integrate the Braun business category between October and December as planned, we risked hurting Braun's sales for the entire year.

For context, it is common in the small appliances industry, which includes Braun, for most of the year's sales to happen during the Christmas season. So if anything were to go wrong in changing the systems for accounting, HR, IT, and sales, it would affect the entire year's performance. The last quarter of the year was simply not a good time to cut over systems. Hence, when viewed in isolation, it might have seemed like a no-brainer to reschedule the Braun cutover. However, the bigger picture was more complex. Sticking to the individual business unit systems' cutover plans was core to delivering on schedule the entire Gillette acquisition synergy targets.

The Gillette Company Acquisition Context

When P&G acquired Gillette for $57Bn in 2005, the stock market's reaction was fairly positive. Warren Buffett, the largest shareholder at Gillette, called it a "dream deal." However, industry statistics record that between 70% and 90% of all acquisitions and divestitures struggle to deliver their synergy goals. P&G's stock fell a modest 2% upon the announcement. It was paramount to deliver cost synergies rapidly.

P&G committed itself to delivering cost synergies of more than $1.2Bn a year, starting within three years. This implied that the combined operations, especially those in supporting functions, would be able to operate in a significantly leaner fashion. Integrating business processes and systems was therefore critical. However, this would be a daunting task. Integrating all business processes, ranging from supply chain to sales to finance and so on, within a couple of years was extremely challenging. This pace of change was necessary so that the cost synergy benefit would be accrued quickly, but this had never been done before at this scale. All the business processes of a $10Bn company, affecting all countries in the world, would need to be completely integrated for this to work. P&G's GBS organization would lead this project for the company, with participation from all functions and business units from both companies. Given the high stakes, project sponsorship came from the very top. A highly detailed project plan to schedule this change was created. This wasn't going to be ideal or convenient, given the narrow window within which all this change had to occur. But the schedule was firmly agreed to. And then about nine months later, when the business process change began to be executed for Braun, the sales risk question came up. Swapping out all the sales, accounting, IT, and HR systems during the busiest sales season of the year would be like changing car tires while driving.

Managing by Fellowship on the Gillette Cutover Issue

As business process change leaders, we had several options for addressing this question. The easiest, in some way, would be to exert a mandate for change. These plans had been committed to about a year earlier. Opening the window for one business unit to replan could trigger a host of other businesses to suggest changing their plans too. Moreover, the Braun business unit knew about the importance of the Christmas season when the original plans were drawn up. Replanning the integration would mean backing away from Wall Street commitments that had been made on synergy. All of this suggested that there were valid arguments to steamroll over Braun's objections. But that wouldn't be optimal decision-making.

So instead, we applied management by fellowship. First, the process change leaders for all functions (finance, HR, etc.) were embedded and made equal partners with the Braun team members in the integration project team. That made it possible to examine together the pros and cons of delaying the change. Second, the structure of "client management" from GBS into the Braun business unit was already in place. That allowed strategic-level conversations to occur within the Braun leadership team. Third, the cost and benefit would be measurable. Early in the project, it had been determined that each day's acceleration or delay in the overall schedule would be the equivalent of swinging $3M of the committed $1.2Bn synergy goal. So, would delaying the Braun cutover to minimize sales risk be better than accepting a confirmed loss of $3M per day on synergies?

The answer was amicably agreed to—we would proceed as originally scheduled. The actual decision itself is less important to our story than the way it was arrived at. Getting the CEOs of the two companies to agree to mandate the original schedule could have been attempted. But influencing the organization to arrive at the right decision, based on specific and aligned-to principles, as well as clear business measures, is always better.

The Learning from Gillette's Integration: Create Movements by Fellowship

The truth is there's never a convenient time to introduce process change within an organization.

Of course, a change can always be executed based on an immediate burning issue. That's possible. It's also possible to find a "less inconvenient" time for the process change to occur. But a convenient time? Forget it. By definition, any change that could destabilize internal operations is a lower priority than delivering this year's sales and profits. It's the difference between the *important* and the *urgent*. So it's not surprising that in general, process changes are viewed with the same enthusiasm as a root canal.

Now add to this mix the gaps in commercialization skills, as mentioned in the previous chapter. The result is usually a case for change in the business process that's about as convincing as a plea for regular dental flossing.

Let's add a third data point: the most common challenge cited by business process transformation leaders is lack of a leadership mandate. Well, let's examine that further, at the risk of beating to death our analogy of "dentists versus transformation leaders." There's no denying that the life of a dentist would be much easier if there existed a higher-order mandate for good oral hygiene. But a mandate doesn't exist for dentists, and it's wishful thinking to expect one for business process transformation leaders. In fact, should a mandate be enforced, it would potentially be counterproductive. Most of the time, mandates generate antibodies, by the sheer nature of the mandate. Reactions range from passive resistance to open opposition to lack of engagement and contribution.

So, how do you exercise proactive leadership for perpetual process changes if it feels like you're constantly pulling teeth? The answer is: by exerting influence without direct authority or, as we think about it, managing by fellowship. In a complex modern organization, it's increasingly common that your impact is defined more by *how* you wield influence rather than by the size of your budget or organization. That is why managing by influence is increasingly being called the only skill that every manager needs.[55]

How Managing by Fellowship Helps Scale Change

Traditional leadership skills have often overemphasized the more straightforward styles, such as:

- Inspirational Leadership
- Delegative Leadership
- Authoritative Leadership
- Transactional Leadership
- Transformational Leadership

These styles are easy to comprehend, though not necessarily easy to develop. However, the bigger problem is that as organizations become more complex, matrixed, and interdependent, these leadership styles become insufficient. Their primary limitation relates to the ability to drive exponential scale and to self-perpetuate.

So it has become necessary to add another tool to the leadership arsenal: the skill to deliver results without having direct control of resources. That new leadership style has been variously called "participative leadership" or "managing by influence." Applying participative leadership for dynamic business process transformation requires a model. We call ours "managing by fellowship."

The Model: Lead by Fellowship

So, how does this model help to scale change? And is this a skill set that can be developed so that business process leaders can create lasting culture movements?

1. **Articulate compelling ideas:** Let's start by clarifying that this isn't just about creating a vision, no matter how strong it may be. That's certainly a good start. But beyond that, we need a clear and compelling set of ideas on how exactly we'll achieve our vision. Contrast that with how most companies articulate their business process projects: "We're going to upgrade our ERP," or we're "Implementing a new CRM system." Even when specific business processes and benefits are mentioned, they're often articulated as fuzzy visions like "Supply Chain of the Future." Instead, why not label our "Analytics and Dashboarding Project" with a term that clarifies the benefits, such as "Steering the Business in Real Time." Calling our vision for master data quality improvement something like "One Touch Master Data" is much more descriptive of the end state and value creation, and therefore more energizing.

2. **Create communities:** There are communities with a big "C" and those with a small "c." The big-C communities are formal structures that often amount to toothless committees: "Community of Practice [COP] for User Experience," or "COP for Advanced Analytics." These communities primarily share knowledge or set standards. They are more akin to learning institutions than to movements. That's not the *community* we have in mind. The communities we would like to build (let's call them the small-c communities) are ecosystems created for very clear "use cases," to *execute* compelling visions. The best examples are successful intrapreneurship programs like GE's Fastworks and Cisco's Innovate Everywhere Challenge. GE's Fastworks[56] helped generate ideas from employees on improving daily activities, ranging from how to fund projects to how to conduct annual reviews. Cisco sought innovative ideas from employees and used a venture capital model to sort through the best ones. Creative processes like these can

change the culture. They support subliminal messages around innovation and open-market behavior while improving the quality of business processes.

3. **Build credibility:** To get mass movement on big process improvements, it's important to start with a strong foundation of credibility. Employees will look at our actions rather than our words to figure out whether this is a corporate power grab or a genuine commitment to the idea. So, what should we do? First, get our own house in order. If we're championing a movement on "lights out" or "defectless" IT operations, and our current IT services are of suspect quality, then we're not going to convince others to join a movement. Second, put the goals of the movement above personal benefit. If Gandhi could accept jail terms so that the bigger freedom movement would benefit, then we can certainly forgo personal corporate recognition or reward. Finally, show results. A movement that cannot show results is seen as a quixotic adventure.

4. **Embrace diverse opinions:** Movements work when the leader fulfills an unmet need. In the context of creating business process movements, the stakeholders are clear. We have the users, the clients, and the subject matter experts. We need to be open to input from all three. If we want to create a movement to get to a vision of "touchless orders and payments" in the order-to-cash business process, then our role in creating a movement is to ensure that we're designing for input from all the stakeholders. Success in this vision isn't going to be driven by a brilliant individual working alone. Working with all three groups of stakeholders is critical to sustaining the movement.

These four skills—(1) articulating compelling ideas, (2) creating communities, (3) building credibility, and (4) embracing diverse opinions—help create a virtuous circle of fellowship. A compelling idea, made available to a community, led by a credible figure who respects and promotes different opinions, is what leads to a movement. Business process movements can then change the culture of the organization from the inside.

Checklist Items for Stage 4, *Unified Accountability*

To strengthen *Unified Accountability*, compare performance with the following Stage 4 characteristics.

- ☑ Business operations leaders drive business change proactively and effectively, influencing culture beyond organization boundaries.

- ☑ They are seen by the business units and functions as the "go-to" partners for wicked problems and opportunities. They take ownership and accountability for business results.

- ☑ Business operations show strong leadership at all levels. They are credible and highly respected for their business knowledge and ability to manage by influence.

- ☑ Effective communication is an integral skill of the business operations organization. It can articulate compelling business ideas and create strong fellowship across the business community.

- ☑ Business operations show a strong business transformation mindset and skill set. They generate consistently new and big ideas through strong collaboration with the business.

Creating a Dynamic Organizational DNA

KEY INSIGHT: An organization's culture, which is its DNA, dictates every action. We can learn from biological DNA editing about how to engineer desired organizational culture changes.

What is the ultimate, self-perpetuating business process design? Obviously, it isn't a specific technology or some other single-point-in-time solution. We are looking for something that reinvents itself over time. The only possible path to perpetual self-improvement is linked to the organization's DNA. Processes, systems, and structures have limited shelf lives; it is the *people* and the *culture* that can drive continual excellence. At the Stage 4 maturity level for *sustained* competitive advantage, we need to add tool sets for "dynamic DNA" to the driver of *Dynamic Operating Engine*. That will deliver the model for a culture that is constantly self-improving.

But, Can You Change an Organization's DNA?

Your organization's culture is its DNA.[57] It is the internal foundation that influences every activity in the organization. It is widespread, it is long-lasting, and it guides the behavior of every person. Consequently, the term Corporate DNA (or Organizational DNA), a metaphor based on biological DNA, has become popular over the past few decades. Booz & Company[58] went as far as to identify the four bases of Organizational DNA (Structure, Decision Rights, Motivators, and Information), deriving them from the four biological DNA bases: adenine (A), guanine (G), cytosine (C), and thymine (T). In living organisms the DNA informs and directs everything that happens to each cell in the body; in just the same way, Organizational DNA dictates every action in an organization. But DNA change is extremely difficult. Biological DNA change happens slowly, either through environmental factors or from progenitor to offspring. Which leads us to this question: can we really change the DNA of an organization? The answer can draw from the biological DNA metaphor: we can change the Organizational DNA quite deliberately by changing the environmental factors and/or the leadership heredity.

The Story of Gene Editing inside a Living Person

In February 2020, the Casey Eye Institute in Portland, Oregon,[59] performed the first gene editing surgical procedure inside a living human being, to prevent blindness from a known genetic mutation. The technology used was CRISPR, which after a decade of research is now being used in myriad applications to edit DNA. CRISPR stands for Clustered Regularly Interspaced Short Palindromic Repeat, which refers to the organization of certain DNA sequences. The technology is designed to locate a specific piece of DNA inside a cell and replace it, in much the same way that you might cut and paste text in, say, Microsoft Word. CRISPR had been used several times to edit human DNA; what made this a unique moment in history was that this was the first gene editing procedure carried out *inside* a living person, in all of medicine. All previous procedures had involved genes being edited in a lab *outside* the living organism.

The genetic disease that was treated this way is called retinal dystrophy. It manifests itself over time with side effects such as colorblindness or tunnel vision and can lead to complete blindness. According

---

Why Engineered DNA Change Is Important

The technique of CRISPR-Cas9 is a once-in-a-lifetime scientific development that has rapidly led to DNA editing applications like the following:

- Addressing diseases like cancer, heart disease, Lyme disease, sickle cell anemia, and Alzheimer's
- Eliminating swine influenza, which costs the world billions of dollars annually
- Curing malaria by changing mosquito DNA
- Developing pig organ transplants for humans
- Producing cheap mass-produced biofuels

There are dozens of other applications, which include more exotic cases like resurrecting the woolly mammoth, reverse engineering the interim species within evolution that led one branch of dinosaurs to evolve into birds, and ... creating hangover-free alcohol.

---

to Dr. Eric Pierce, leader of the clinical trial study, "If one of the genes needed for vision is misspelled, the cells get sick and die. The goal of this procedure is to fix the correct spelling of one of the misspelled genes that causes degeneration, which would, in turn, allow the cells to restore their health and restore vision."

The Various Ways in Which Biological DNA Can Change

This procedure was a first, but it is hardly the only example of DNA change. In daily life, changes to DNA happen every time an organism gives birth. The result is referred to as germline DNA because it comes from the parent DNA and can be passed on to the child. Then there's somatic or acquired DNA mutation. That's caused by environmental factors ranging from ultraviolet radiation from the sun to smoke from cigarettes, diseases like cancer, or simply errors in copying DNA during cell division. The third way to change DNA is the genome-editing technique CRISPR—more accurately, CRISPR-Cas9 (Cas9 stands for

"CRISPR-associated protein 9"). The Cas9 protein sniffs out the exact genes, then the CRISPR makes the change.

The point is that biological DNA change was once considered to be slow-moving and not controllable. Today, though, it is viewed as fair game for rapid CRISPR-Cas9 modifications. Is there an equivalent engineered-change mechanism for Corporate DNA? The existing dogma has been that corporate culture is slow to change. However, we believe we can take lessons from how biological DNA editing has been accelerated.

Learning from Biological DNA Editing:
Some Key Factors Can Be Reapplied to Organizational DNA

We mentioned the study that identified the four bases of Organizational DNA (Structure, Decision Rights, Motivators, and Information), which were metaphorically built on the four biological DNA bases: adenine (A), guanine (G), cytosine (C), and thymine (T). Let's go deeper for lessons on how to edit Organizational DNA. The work on CRISPR-Cas9 offers three organizational insights:

1. **DNA is an outcome of design and environmental forces:**
    Biological DNA is made up of chemical elements (called nucleotides), which include the bases A-G-C-T. It can be inherited or modified by the environment. The biological DNA itself is an outcome of these forces of design and the environment. That's true of Organizational DNA too. Since we can only build it based on inherited traits and environmental factors, we can "edit" Organizational DNA by changing these factors of design and the environment.

2. **We need different DNA edits for different purposes:** The CRISPR edits needed for retinal dystrophy are very different from those related to sickle cell disease. Similarly, the Organizational DNA changes needed for dynamic business process transformation will be different from those needed for,

say, effective product innovation. We will focus here on business operations excellence.

3. **The use cases are many, but the base units of DNA are few:** Finally, the most exciting insight: while DNA edit uses are plentiful, the bases always come back to the A-G-C-T sequence. The implication, if we use the Booz and Company bases of Structure, Decision Rights, Motivators, and Information, is that we can act on these to create our individual DNA for dynamic business process transformation by editing these four. The challenge then becomes to identify the specific modifications to these four bases.

Our experience of helping dozens of organizations change their Organization DNA tells us that these three simple insights can help us modify the four Organization DNA bases: Structure, Decision Rights, Motivators, and Information, as elaborated in the next section. The exciting result is the creation of the ultimate, self-perpetuating business process design.

The Model: How to Create a Dynamic Organizational DNA

We can change the four bases in specific ways to create a dynamic Organizational DNA. For Stage 4 maturity, each of the bases needs to change in specific ways, which are outlined in Figure 16.

1. Structure: From Stability to Speedy Execution

By the end of the Stage 3 maturity of dynamic business process transformation, we had created an organization model that was streamlined and centralized and that had been made customer-centric via client management and relevant metrics. It was fine-tuned to operate efficiently, effectively, innovatively, and with the customer's best interests at heart. The internal business process operations could deliver best-in-class financial, HR, supply chain, finance, IT, R&D, and marketing operations. It had taken the organization some time to adapt to the

DNA BASES	FROM	TO
Structure	Stability	Speedy execution
Decision Rights	Role clarity	Role empowerment
Motivators	Generic reward systems	Business-centric motivators
Information	Info for operations	Info for change

FIGURE 16: Organization DNA Changes

new structure, individual role expectations, and the new design of daily operations.

Well, from this position of strength, it's time to fine-tune it again.

That may seem like a lot to take on, or unnecessary, but this is what differentiates good from great organizations. This relentless quest to evolve is necessary not just to effectively manage environmental changes in the business but also to create new disruptive business processes for competitive advantage. At Procter & Gamble's GBS, we set up an internal expectation that the organization would be redesigned every two or three years. This started with centralizing and offshoring most business process operations around the world. It was followed three years later with organizing to run business processes as if these were open market businesses. That included outsourcing two-thirds of the back-office work. A few years later, the bar was raised so as to drive more business process innovation while reducing costs as a percentage of sales by one-third. Finally, this evolved into operating GBS as a transformation engine for the enterprise, with digital and business process transformation becoming paramount for the company. Then came the creation of industry-shaping next-generation services, which created products that benchmarked with startups rather than big companies.

Here's the point, though: each of these structure evolutions was proactive, not reactive. It wasn't done as a response to an environmental change, but in anticipation of that change. Each change was intended to make the organization even better and faster, no matter how good we were by traditional benchmarks. We were self-driven and self-adapting. Equally important, the organization started to expect it. Change leadership becomes easier when the organization itself starts to ask, "Isn't it time to change again?" This is, by itself, an Organizational DNA change.

2. Decision Rights: From Role Clarity to Role Empowerment

The big idea, at this stage of maturity, is empowerment of individuals within their given roles, whether they involve process operations, service management, or client management. The inherent problem with business process management, even more so than with product management, is that the total number of internal stakeholders is high. If we want to change the source-to-pay process, we likely need to line up not just the procurement function but also finance, IT, supply chain, and vendors, not to mention the business units themselves. There is a proven approach to empowering process organization roles like service managers. It involves getting the best performance out of not just the service managers but each of the many stakeholders as well. Here are the steps involved:

a. Empower and openly declare E2E service manager accountability.

b. Ensure that all stakeholders understand what their contribution is and hold them to their promises.

c. Role-model empowerment personally by avoiding overmanagement.

d. Break up outcomes into clear and short-cycle objectives.

3. Motivators: From Generic Reward Systems to Business-Specific Motivators

For employees who work on business processes, it is important to link their *main* reward system to self-perpetuating business process improvements. Start by deriving a part of the employee's performance metrics from a common business goal. That could be shareholder return (which in turn is driven by revenue growth, profitability, and asset efficiency), or member impact in the case of not-for-profit organizations, or similar. Most organizations have general corporate rewards for such things as customer focus, going above and beyond, business building ideas, and so on. However, when applied to employees whose focus is on internal business process operations, they deliver limited results. Generic motivational rewards, such as for "unparalleled collaboration," are too fuzzy and therefore not tied strongly enough to business outcomes.

4. Information: From Info for Operations to Info for Change

Most business processes don't evolve constantly because it is hard to work in an operations mode and a transformation mode at the same time. For example, if your job as a social media community manager requires you to constantly stay on top of all communications, you may be drained by the end of the day. Thinking about strategies to disrupt social media requires a deliberate change of pace and block of time carved out for refocusing.

Embracing the opposing forces between daily operations and transformational change is key to a self-perpetuating excellent operation. The best leaders in the world hold two opposing ideas in fruitful tension, then integrate the best of both. This phenomenon was researched and written up by Roger Martin in his book *Opposable Minds*,[60] which builds on the metaphor of opposable thumbs. Opposable role expectations are a necessity; indeed, they are a game changer, not just for executives but at the operations level as well. That isn't always brought to life. Currently, for most operations-related positions, the information targeted at the employee mostly relates to their core job—for example, dashboards of performance for their business process. It's important to design information sharing and communications to employees in a manner that constantly highlights both types of information.

Combined, these four "edits" introduce specific changes to the Organization DNA to deliver an ongoing competitive advantage based on business processes. Not being deliberate about editing the Organization DNA to create a desired culture of self-change can be risky. By the way, ignoring the perils of organization culture is a trap that even highly skilled experts can stumble into. For instance, in evaluating stock prices correctly, or assessing the risks of mergers and acquisitions, it can be possible to underrepresent the importance of organization culture. The largest merger in American business history is a case in point. The AOL–Timer Warner merger was valued at $350Bn in 2000; nine years later, it had collapsed. It remains a textbook example of the consequences of underappreciating clashing Organization DNAs.

Fortunately, for every AOL–Time Warner, there's a Google, or P&G, or Starbucks. In our experience, zooming into the "edits" necessary for sustained business process advantage via the four base Organizational DNA items works consistently. There are new models that help you identify changes in Structure, Decision Rights, Motivators, and Information. By coordinating these, it is possible to create the ultimate, self-perpetuating business process design.

Checklist Items for Stage 4, *Dynamic Operating Engine*

To strengthen the *Dynamic Operating Engine*, compare performance with the following Stage 4 characteristics.

- ☑ The business operations organization displays strong leadership at all touch points with the business. It's motivated and driven by business-centric outcomes.

- ☑ Business processes continue to evolve, be innovated, and be transformed through strong and widespread change management capabilities.

- ☑ The organization culture shows specific traits: highly proactive, empowered to drive change, highly agile, and responsive. There is a "quest to be the best" in business-centricity and value creation.

☑ The "DNA" of the business operations organization changes dynamically, based on evolving business needs. The interaction with the business is at the core and deemed best-in-class.

☑ Financial performance, operational excellence, and the building of new business capabilities are in excellent balance and constantly adjusted as needed.

PART VI

Achieving
Competitive Advantage
via Business Operations

The Full *Dynamic Process Transformation* Model

Action Steps for *Dynamic Process Transformation*

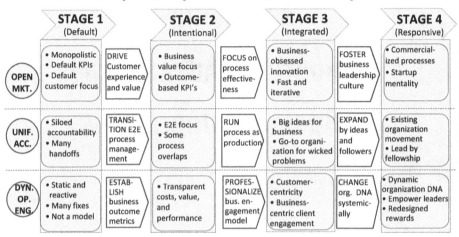

	STAGE 1 (Default)		STAGE 2 (Intentional)		STAGE 3 (Integrated)		STAGE 4 (Responsive)
OPEN MKT.	• Monopolistic • Default KPIs • Default customer focus	DRIVE Customer experience and value	• Business value focus • Outcome-based KPI's	FOCUS on process effectiveness	• Business-obsessed innovation • Fast and iterative	FOSTER business leadership culture	• Commercial-ized processes • Startup mentality
UNIF. ACC.	• Siloed accountability • Many handoffs	TRANSITION E2E process management	• E2E focus • Some process overlaps	RUN process as production	• Big ideas for business • Go-to organization for wicked problems	EXPAND by ideas and followers	• Existing organization movement • Lead by fellowship
DYN. OP. ENG.	• Static and reactive • Many fixes • Not a model	ESTABLISH business outcome metrics	• Transparent costs, value, and performance	PROFESSIONALIZE bus. engagement model	• Customer-centricity • Business-centric client engagement	CHANGE org. DNA systemically	• Dynamic organization DNA • Empower leaders • Redesigned rewards

What is the full model for *Dynamic Process Transformation*?

The end goal of *Dynamic Process Transformation* is to create an ever-evolving set of business processes that dynamically change without the need for episodic jolts of one-off transformations. The focus of this section is to help you create your own plans for implementing this.

Actions to increase maturity from one stage to the next

- VISION for a compelling end state

- GOALS to measure progress

- STRATEGIES on which choices are best suited to get you there

- INITIATIVES to deliver the change in a planned manner

FIGURE 17: Action Steps for *Dynamic Process Transformation*

15

How to Succeed in
Dynamic Process Transformation

KEY INSIGHT: The most important ingredient of this transformation is you!

We have intended this book to be an *applied* guide to revolutionizing business operations. In that vein, we'd like to suggest how you might use the insights from this book on your own journey to *Dynamic Process Transformation*. But before we jump into the steps on that journey, we'd like to make a point we feel strongly about. The winning ingredient for revolutionizing business operations is not the *Dynamic Process Transformation* model itself, however many insights it offers, nor is it even the new process designs; it is a *person*—that is, *you*. It takes an individual's vision and personal leadership to catalyze and deliver change. Whether the organization is open to change, or the journey will be a slog, are secondary questions. We will never know for sure until a leader takes the first step at the head of that journey. We hope this book has provided enough information for you to seize the day. So, as you accept the challenge to do that, here are the four steps on the journey.

STEP 1: **Vision**   STEP 3: **Strategies**

STEP 2: **Goals**   STEP 4: **Initiatives**

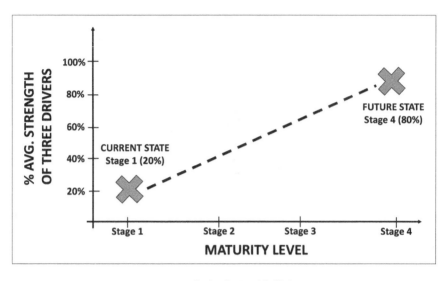

FIGURE 18: Goals—Start and End Points

STEP 1: Vision
Imagine the Future

Imagining what revolutionary operations could look like in the future within a specific organization isn't easy. Oh, it's easy enough to capture a couple of statements on the vision, or to groupthink on a generic vision of delivering competitive advantage, or being the most cost-effective and agile operation, or maximizing business value. That's not what we are talking about. We need something that will light a fire in our bellies, something that is meaningful to our organization, something that will become a movement over time. One approach is to think about how this vision could become the backbone for delivering the company's *purpose*. So, to use Patagonia as an example, since their company vision is "To use all of its resources to defend life on earth," our hypothetical operations vision could aspire to maximize the company's resources by being highly responsive, efficient, and innovative in supporting life on earth.

STEP 2: Goals
Identify the Starting and Ending Points of the Transformation

To set the goal, we suggest using the four stages of maturity from this book and measuring the strength of the drivers. The four maturity stages of *default, intentional, integrated,* and *responsive* will tell you what needs to be achieved. This needs to be complemented on a second axis with a measure of improvement in the three drivers of *Open Market Rules, Unified Accountability,* and *Dynamic Operating Engine.* This second axis thus represents the percentage strength of the three drivers combined. As illustrated in Figure 18, we share an example of the starting and ending points of the transformation going from Stage 1 (20% strength) to Stage 4 (80% strength). Our website www.RBO-book.com provides more resources to help you do this.

STEP 3: Strategies
Identify the Choices Needed to Get There

Chapters 3 to 14 outlined the action steps for progressing on the four maturity stages and the three drivers. Some combination of these ideas will be needed to get to the end state. Figure 17, provided at the beginning of Part VI, describes the characteristics of the four stages in the vertical columns, with the strategies for progressing from one point to the next in chevrons. You can use that figure as an inspiration for creating tailored strategies. Workshopping the development of these would be a good idea.

STEP 4: Initiatives
Define the Projects or Programs to Be Executed

At some point, all the activities needed to transform business operations can be boiled down into changing either organization structures, processes, rewards, or information systems. At this step, we translate the strategies defined previously into project plans for these four items. This will require involving as many stakeholders and organization members as possible.

These steps of vision, goals, strategies, and initiatives may sound linear, but that isn't our intention. You will need to review and adapt them, either as part of the annual strategy cycle of the organization or as needed. In a dynamic world, you must stay responsive to changes in the business context. Everything you do, whether you are evolving your process operations or the strategies themselves, must be viewed through this lens. Therefore, as we conclude this book, we'd like to zoom back from the specific actions in order to reinforce this broader picture. You need to constantly evolve from yesterday's thinking and focus on where the future lies.

Move Away from Yesterday's Logic

Peter Drucker, the management guru, said, "The greatest danger in times of turbulence is not the turbulence—it is to act with yesterday's logic." That has never been more true. Yesterday's logic said that every business process—whether accounting, order management, or selling—had an ideal design. Yesterday's logic convinced us that there were IT systems that could closely mimic and automate that ideal state. Yesterday's logic dictated that competitive advantage could come mainly from superior products and that internal business processes were usually the cost of doing business.

That's an outdated mindset. To be fair, it was a sufficient mindset for the pre-information era. Streamlining business processes, standardizing and automating them, and managing them end-to-end, absolutely did optimize them—for that point in time. These *static* business process transformation programs were effective for a few years after completion, but only in the same sense that a diet regimen delivers results for some amount of time. Until, that is, the environment changes.

What has altered in recent years is the speed of change in the business environment. To keep up, we need not one-off (static) but perpetual (dynamic) business process transformation. We require not just the best diet regimen, but a personal lifestyle change. As we learned early in the book from the three case studies of Francisco Fraga, Yazdi Bagli, and Caroline Basyn, businesses can no longer afford the time or the cost of periodic large transformation programs. It takes personal leadership to change yesterday's logic, as these executives did by leveraging the three drivers.

Connect the Dots to Seize the Opportunity

We know the *Dynamic Process Transformation* model works. That has been proven in different contexts. But that's not the issue. The question is, how can *you* go about applying it?

When we, the authors, started our business operations careers more than three decades ago, the model for success seemed easy—standardize, simplify, and automate. However, having achieved global best-in-class status a decade later, it felt like we were back at square one. Our efficiency- and effectiveness-driving strategies could be carried out equally well by outsourcing to external business process partners. What, then, was distinctive about our role?

For roughly the next decade, our distinctiveness resided in our business-centricity and innovation. No external party could understand our company's needs or innovate better than we could. So, innovate is what we did next. It worked extremely well for many years, until the world changed again.

With the onset of the fourth industrial revolution, the very definition of competition and industry structure changed. What was an internet company was potentially also a consumer-packaged goods competitor. It was a different game. Business operations now needed the agility of a startup because startups were the new competition.

Today, yet again, the context has changed. It's no longer just startup-like agility that counts. In this fourth era, what matters is agility, *plus* the personalization to win each customer, *plus* doing things at scale.

It's important to connect the dots across all these trends. There will be a fifth, and a sixth, and a seventh era. Each successive era will be shorter. There will be less time and fewer resources to do each transformation program. We must be clear-eyed about the challenge. One-off (static) transformations are simply inadequate for the future. We need dynamic business process transformations. Not seeing the forest for the trees could be a costly mistake.

We encourage you to avoid this. We challenge you to leverage personal leadership to grasp the changing context and to create your own approaches for revolutionizing business operations. The upside is immense. Imagine not having to reevaluate your distinctive skills and your competitive advantage every few years. What if you never had to worry about the fate of your business or your job because you were always a step ahead? With the hindsight of seeing business operations evolve, and then evolve again, we're convinced that this is possible.

It is said that destiny finds those who listen, and fate finds the rest. Are you ready to shape your own destiny?

Authors' note: Find more information and contribute to the growing knowledge base on the *Dynamic Process Transformation* model at RBO-book.com. We look forward to input and feedback and to responding to your questions there.

Revolutionizing Business Operations

DISCUSSION GUIDE

This guide is meant for executives, operations leaders, consultants, teachers, and students who want to apply the *Dynamic Process Transformation* model. To tailor the discussion to specific situations, we have organized questions for two different personas—executives/consultants and teachers/students.

Discussion Guide for Company Executives and External Consultants

The following sets of questions are intended to guide your learning and to help you make choices about dynamic business operations. They could be used for personal reflection or group discussion. They are organized to help you explore why and how you might approach *Dynamic Process Transformation.*

Why Revolutionize Business Operations?

As you think about the need to revolutionize the operations of your own organization or your client's, consider the following questions.

1. What is the purpose of the organization's operations? How well is it serving its customers today? And how well is it positioned to keep serving in the future?

2. Are there specific outcomes (e.g., business, customer, societal, environmental, or organizational) that are most vulnerable? How might you articulate and measure the success of the transformation?

3. How dynamic is the organization (in terms of skills, methodologies, and empowerment). Is it dynamic enough to adapt to changing needs?

4. Who among the operation's clients and key stakeholders would agree that dynamic processes need to be built? Who would actively disagree?

5. What are your biggest concerns about revolutionizing business operations?

Open Market Rules Questions

The *Open Market Rules* driver is intended to keep the business processes adaptable to changing business, customer, and environmental needs. The opportunity here is to create continuous new value for the business and to turn operations into a competitive advantage.

1. Are business operations run with a mindset of "winning in the open market," rather than catering to internal "back office" or commodity needs?

2. Is there relentless focus on the user, the stakeholder, and the customer? This is not just declared or a good intention, but diligently measured.

3. Does the organization constantly and constructively challenge the status quo, to find ever new ways to bring distinctive value?

4. Do the performance measures include customer value, as deemed important by the customer? These may range from ease of use to better experience or new capabilities.

5. Is innovation for process operations applied systemically, through the consistent and broad-based application of frameworks (Design Thinking, Lean Startup, Agile)?

Unified Accountability Questions

Given the siloed origins of business processes, it is vital to establish clear accountability for E2E processes. This goes way beyond E2E GPO roles. There must be *Unified Accountability* for standards, outcomes, employees, and budgets.

1. Are all business processes run as "products," with centralized accountability? Is there great consistency in the skill sets and tools being applied?

2. Are service managers appointed to run processes end-to-end and holistically? Do those processes reflect cost, feedback, KPIs, quality, and ongoing transformation?

3. Has a process catalog been defined, bringing strong transparency and clarity to the users and stakeholders?

4. Are we sure there is absolutely no confusion about who is in charge, and empowered, to drive continuous improvement to the individual processes?

5. Has the accountability for process innovation been clarified? Is it exercised effectively? And does it play out at all levels in the organization?

Dynamic Operating Engine Questions

The best way to ensure that business operations become predictably excellent and keep evolving to stay that way is to operate from a robust model. Many business process organizations don't have an operating engine that includes professional approaches to operations, continuous improvement, customer-centricity, innovation, and financial management.

1. Is there a standard and robust operating model in the operations organization? Is it designed to constantly detect needed changes and swiftly respond accordingly?

2. Are there clear metrics in place, totally aligned, documented, and regularly validated? Is there often some confusion with regard to value creation?

3. Are business operations' "client managers" embedded in the business and an integral part of the business unit leadership team?

4. Does the organization culture show specific traits: highly proactive, empowered to drive change, highly agile, and responsive? Is there a quest to be the best in business-centricity and value creation?

5. Does the "DNA" of the business operations organization change dynamically based on evolving business needs? Is interaction with the business at the core and deemed best-in-class?

Discussion Guide for Teachers and Students

The following discussion topics are structured to help teachers and students discuss why dynamic business transformation is necessary and how to approach it. We suggest using the questions to brainstorm the opportunities and threats presented by the four stages of maturity.

Why and How *Dynamic Process Transformation* Is Done

Business processes were historically viewed as the cost of running a product or service organization. With the advent of digital technology, it is now evident that *how* we run an operation can make a difference when it comes to beating the competition. The following questions serve as a guide for reflecting on how to transform business operations so that they become a winning asset.

1. How has the role of business operations evolved over the years? And how does it vary with the type of organization (e.g., private company versus public, or large organization versus small)?

2. To what degree are the outcomes (e.g., business, customer, societal, environmental, or organizational) directly impacted by outdated processes and operations? How might we articulate and measure the size of the prize for transforming them?

3. What are the various ways in which an organization's capabilities (in terms of skills, methodologies, and empowerment) should adapt to the changing needs of customers?

4. Why would some of the operation's clients and key stakeholders agree that dynamic processes need to be built? Why would some of them disagree?

Stage 1 (Default) Maturity Questions

All business processes evolve in line with their organization structures. As functional organizations support processes for business units or geographies, they evolve independently. Stage 1 maturity processes are usually characterized as "back-office" and thus monopolistic in culture. There isn't a consistent model across business processes for operations, or for optimizing them. Here are questions to ponder.

1. Given the siloed and monopolistic nature of business processes, what are the best strategies for driving internal customer experience and value?

2. Why and how would functional leaders who "own" business processes be open to transitioning to E2E process management?

3. How might we go about establishing E2E process metrics that are based on business outcomes?

Stage 2 (Intentional) Maturity Questions

At Stage 2, the operation has already evolved toward being more E2E in managing processes. The intent is to go beyond delivering efficiency so as to become more effective. Performance metrics (KPIs) are outcome-based and factor in customer experience, built around transparency and business value creation. Here are the discussion items at this stage.

1. If the business process organizations are delivering efficient and low-cost operations, then what are the key levers for creating further business value?

2. In what ways is running business processes similar to managing product groups? In what ways is it different?

3. What processes do professional account managers employ to effectively engage with and deliver value to their clients? And to what extent can this be used within internal business process service delivery?

Stage 3 (Integrated) Maturity Questions

Once business processes become efficient as well as effective, the next step is to make them innovative. Business processes can be continuously innovated on, just like any product. At this level of maturity, innovation is prioritized in terms of financial and customer value. Here are the suggested questions for discussion.

1. How might we foster a culture of business leadership within the process organization? What types of opportunities can transform processes and add value?

2. What are the ways in which product companies innovate? How can process organizations learn from this?

3. What behaviors and outcomes do process organizations typically reward? How will those need to be tweaked if our expectation is that process teams need to innovate in addition to delivering efficient services?

Stage 4 (Responsive) Maturity Questions

The final frontier is to establish an Organization DNA that is self-disrupting. In a Stage 4 organization, change agents operate at all levels, sharing a common mindset, skill set, and tool set. The operating models blend a startup mentality with rigorous, reliable, and ever-improving operations. Here are the questions.

1. Since most process organizations cannot directly control all inputs and outputs of their process, what are the best ways to manage by influence? Are there parallel examples of roles that must use this style of leadership?

2. What are some ideas to drive higher adoption and even more value out of existing processes? Is there an equivalent to commercialization or products in the process world?

3. In what ways might we build skills and mindsets within process organizations so that they become self-disruptive and more startup-like?

NOTES

Introduction

1. Shell.com, "Company History," n.d. https://www.shell.com/about-us/our -heritage/our-company-history.html.

2. Leon C. Megginson, "Lessons from Europe for American Business," *Southwestern Social Science Quarterly* (1963) 44(1): 3-13, p. 4.

3. Jennifer Reingold, "P&G Chairman A.G. Lafley Steps Down—for Good, This Time?," *Fortune*, June 2016. https://fortune.com/2016/06/01/pg-chairman-a-g-lafley -steps-down-for-good-this-time.

4. Icmrindia.org, "Procter & Gamble: Organization 2005 and Beyond," n.d. https://www.icmrindia.org/free%20resources/articles/procter3.htm.

5. A.G. Lafley, "What I Learned in the Navy," *Medium*, July 5, 2021. https:// medium.com/@leadingtowin/what-i-learned-in-the-navy-43aa95ea82b0.

Chapter 1

6. Matthias Daub, Andreas Ess, Jonathan Silver, and Samir Singh, "Does the Global Business Services Model Still Matter?," McKinsey & Company, July 13, 2017. https://www.mckinsey.com/business-functions/mckinsey-digital/our-insights/does -the-global-business-services-model-still-matter.

7. Deloitte.com, "2019 Global Shared Services Survey Report 11th Biannual Edition," n.d. https://www2.deloitte.com/content/dam/Deloitte/dk/Documents/strat egy/2019GlobalSharedServicesSurvey_ExecutiveSummary.pdf.

8. Phil Fersht, Tony Filippone, Charles Aird, and Derek Sappenfield, "The Evolution of Global Business Services: Enhancing the Benefits of Shared Services and Outsourcing," Governance Strategies, 2011. https://www.horsesforsources.com/wp -content/uploads/2011/10/HfS-Report-PwC-Developing-Framework-Global-Services -07-2011.pdf.

9. Deloitte Netherlands, "2021 Global Shared Services and Outsourcing Survey Report," May 21, 2021. Deloitte Survey: Global Shared Services and Outsourcing— Press release | Deloitte US.

10. Researchandmarkets.com, "Shared Services: Global Strategic Business

Report," 2020. https://www.researchandmarkets.com/reports/5140291/shared-services-global-strategic-business-report.

Chapter 2

11. Leanproduction.com, "Theory of Constraints (TOC)," n.d. https://www.lean production.com/theory-of-constraints.

Chapter 3

12. Rachel Sanderson, "Poste Italiane on Track with Partial Privatisation This Year," *Financial Times*, September 6, 2015. https://www.ft.com/content/4f3d8348 -5485-11e5-b029-b9d50a74fd14.

13. Giovanni Legorano and Giada Zampano, "Italy Raises $3.8 Billion from Poste IPO," *Wall Street Journal*, October 23, 2015. https://www.wsj.com/articles/italy-raises -3-8-billion-from-poste-ipo-as-part-of-economy-recovery-plans-1445592196.

Chapter 4

14. William Langewiesche, "What Really Happened to Malaysia's Missing Airplane," *The Atlantic*, June 17, 2019. https://www.theatlantic.com/magazine /archive/2019/07/mh370-malaysia-airlines/590653.

15. Pamela Boykoff, "MH370 report: Search delayed by chaos and confusion," CNN, March 9, 2015. https://www.cnn.com/2015/03/09/asia/mh370-report-search -delays/index.html.

16. Bibhudatta Dash and Richelle Deveau, "How quote-to-cash excellence can fuel growth for B2B subscription businesses," McKinsey & Company, October 22, 2020. https://www.mckinsey.com/industries/technology-media-and-telecommunications /our-insights/how-quote-to-cash-excellence-can-fuel-growth-for-b2b-subscription -businesses.

Chapter 5

17. Marli Guzzetta, "The 4 Keys to One of the Biggest Turnarounds in Business History," *Inc.*, October 12, 2017. https://www.inc.com/marli-guzzetta/how-alan -mulally-turned-ford-around-inc5000.html.

18. Marcia Blenko, James Root, and Nader Elkhweet, "When Weak Operating Models Happen to Good Strategy," *Bangkok Post*, April 2, 2015. https://www.bain.com /insights/when-weak-operating-models-happen-to-good-strategy-bangkok-post.

19. Marcia Blenko, James Root, and Nader Elkhweet, "When Weak Operating Models Happen to Good Strategy," *Bangkok Post*, April 7, 2015. https://www.bangkok post.com/business/515723/when-weak-operating-models-happen-to-good-strategy.

20. Rosevear, John, "Ford's Deceptively Simple Strategy," *The Motley Fool*, September 30, 2010. https://www.fool.com/investing/general/2010/09/30/fords -deceptively-simple-strategy.aspx.

21. [Former Member], "List of End to End Business Process in SAP," SAP

Community Blogs, April 17, 2012. https://blogs.sap.com/2012/04/17/list-of-end-to
-end-business-process-in-sap.

Chapter 7

22. UVA Miller Center, "Neil H. McElroy (1957–1959)," October 4, 2016. https://
millercenter.org/president/eisenhower/essays/mcelroy-1957-secretary-of-defense.

23. Martin Eriksson, "The History and Evolution of Product Management," *Mind the Product*, October 28, 2015. https://www.mindtheproduct.com/history-evolution
-product-management.

24. Branding Strategy Insider, "Great Moments in Branding: Neil McElroy Memo," June 12, 2009. https://www.brandingstrategyinsider.com/great-moments-in
-branding-neil-mcelroy-memo.

Chapter 8

25. Kenji Explains, "'Don't Buy This Jacket'—Patagonia's Daring Campaign," *Better Marketing*, June 5, 2020. https://bettermarketing.pub/dont-buy-this-jacket
-patagonia-s-daring-campaign-2b37e145046b.

26. Jamie Gilpin, "Toward a New Model of Business Transparency," *Sprout Social*, September 19, 2018. https://sproutsocial.com/insights/new-model-of-business
-transparency.

27. Tom Swallow, "Patagonia: A Pioneer in the Sustainable Sourcing of Apparel," *sustainabilitymag.com*, December 12, 2021. https://sustainabilitymag.com/esg
/patagonia-pioneer-sustainable-sourcing-apparel.

28. Beth Thoren, "Patagonia Doesn't Use the Word 'Sustainable.' Here's Why," *Fortune*. November 2, 2021. https://fortune.com/2021/11/02/patagonia-doesnt-use
-the-word-sustainable-cop26.

29. "Meet the Company: Patagonia Proves Purpose Can Be Profitable," *business chief.com*, December 2, 2021. https://businesschief.com/sustainability/meet-company
-patagonia-proves-purpose-can-be-profitable.

30. Ryan Smith and Golnaz Tabibnia, "Why Radical Transparency Is Good Business," *Harvard Business Review*, October 11, 2012. https://hbr.org/2012/10/why
-radical-transparency-is-good-business.

Chapter 9

31. "14 Inspiring Examples of Intrapreneurship and Employee Ideas in Action," Sideways6, January 13, 2023. https://ideas.sideways6.com/article/inspiring-examples
-of-intrapreneurship-and-employee-ideas-in-action.

32. Matthew Woodward, "Amazon Prime Statistics: Subscribers, Usage & Revenue 2023," *Search Logistics*, August 31, 2022. https://www.matthewwoodward.co.uk/work
/amazon-prime-statistics.

33. Jason Del Rey, "The Making of Amazon Prime, the Internet's Most Successful

and Devastating Membership Program," *Vox*, May 3, 2019. https://www.vox.com /recode/2019/5/3/18511544/amazon-prime-oral-history-jeff-bezos-one-day-shipping.

34. Amazon Staff, "2017 Letter to Shareholders," April 18, 2018. https://www .aboutamazon.com/news/company-news/2017-letter-to-shareholders.

35. Thoughtworks, "Understanding How Design Thinking, Lean and Agile Work Together," n.d. https://www.thoughtworks.com/insights/blog/understanding-how -design-thinking-lean-and-agile-work-together.

36. ExperiencePoint, "Agile, Lean and Design Thinking: How They Work Together," n.d. https://blog.experiencepoint.com/agile-lean-and-design-thinking-how -they-work-together.

37. ExperiencePoint, "Agile, Lean and Design Thinking: How They Work Together," n.d. https://blog.experiencepoint.com/agile-lean-and-design-thinking-how -they-work-together.

Chapter 10

38. BCG Global, "15 Years of the Most Innovative Companies," n.d. https://www .bcg.com/publications/most-innovative-companies-historical-rankings.

39. "About Samsung," November 11, 2008. https://web.archive.org/web /20110415235250/http://www.samsung.com/us/aboutsamsung/corporateprofile /history06.html.

40. Capitalontap, "The World's Most Innovative Tech Companies." n.d. https:// www.capitalontap.com/en/blog/posts/the-world-s-most-innovative-tech-companies.

41. Ukessays.com, "Samsung Innovation Strategy," July 29, 2022. https://www .ukessays.com/essays/business/samsung-as-a-modern-innovative-organisation -business-essay.php.

42. Bansi Nagji and Geoff Tuff, "Managing Your Innovation Portfolio," *Harvard Business Review*, May 1, 2012. https://hbr.org/2012/05/managing-your-innovation -portfolio.

43. Onova, "Four Examples of Corporate Open Innovation: How Lego, NASA, Samsung, and General Electric Reached New Heights," n.d. https://www.onova.io /innovation-insights/four-examples-of-open-innovation.

44. Abey Francis, "Case Study: Samsung's Innovation Strategy." MBA Knowledge Base, June 16, 2011. https://www.mbaknol.com/business-analysis/case-study-sam sungs-innovation-strategy.

45. Bansi Nagji and Geoff Tuff, "Managing Your Innovation Portfolio." *Harvard Business Review*, May 1, 2012. https://hbr.org/2012/05/managing-your-innovation -portfolio.

Chapter 11

46. Cornerstone International Group, "How P&G Became 'Part of Walmart,'" August 9, 2018. https://www.cornerstone-group.com/2018/08/09/how-pg-became -part-of-walmart.

47. SALESBEAT BLOG, "Walmart and Procter & Gamble," SALESBEAT BLOG, April 8, 2022. https://blog.salesbeat.co/2022/04/08/walmart-and-procter-gamble/.

48. Harvard Business School, "Tom Muccio: Negotiating the P&G Relationship with Wal-Mart (A)," n.d. https://www.hbs.edu/faculty/Pages/item.aspx?num=34008.

Chapter 12

49. Vasan G.S., "Metaverse of Microsoft, Meta, and All the Madness You Need to Know," Smartprix, January 19, 2022. https://www.smartprix.com/bytes/metaverse-explained-everything-you-need-to-know/.

50. Adi Robertson and Jay Peters, "What Is the Metaverse, and Do I Have to Care?," *The Verge*, October 4, 2021. https://www.theverge.com/22701104/metaverse-explained-fortnite-roblox-facebook-horizon.

51. John Watson, "Marketing Vs Commercialization," March 22, 2021. https://accruemarketing.com/marketing-versus-commercialization.

52. Gabriella Daniels, "75% of All System Implementations Fail—Here Is How You Could Succeed," October 8, 2020. https://elearningindustry.com/how-succeed-in-user-adoption-of-new-systems.

53. Thomas H. Davenport, "How P&G Presents Data to Decision-Makers," *Harvard Business Review*, April 4, 2013. https://hbr.org/2013/04/how-p-and-g-presents-data.

Chapter 13

54. David Rock, "The Fastest Way to Change a Culture," *Forbes*, May 24, 2019. https://www.forbes.com/sites/davidrock/2019/05/24/fastest-way-to-change-culture/?sh=6debd1463d50.

55. "Why Managing by Influence Is the Only Skill Every Manager Needs," OpEx Managers, January 10, 2020. https://opexmanagers.com/managing-by-influence.

56. "How 3 Companies Created an Ecosystem for Innovation," innov8rs, n.d. https://innov8rs.co/news/3-companies-created-ecosystem-innovation.

Chapter 14

57. Kenneth Acha, "What Is Organizational DNA?," May 13, 2016. https://www.kennethmd.com/what-is-organizational-dna.

58. Gary L. Neilson, Bruce A. Pasternack, and Decio Mendes. n.d. "The Four Bases of Organizational DNA," n.d. https://www.strategy-business.com/article/03406.

59. OHSU, Casey Eye Institute, "Innovations: Advancing Surgery 2021," 2021. https://www.ohsu.edu/casey-eye-institute/innovations-advancing-surgery-2021.

60. Roger L. Martin, *The Opposable Mind: How Successful Leaders Win through Integrative Thinking* (Cambridge, MA: Harvard Business Review Press, 2009).

ACKNOWLEDGMENTS

In today's disrupted media industry, it's rare to find a publisher who is truly and deeply author-centric. Berrett-Koehler is one of those. Even better, we were lucky to have Steve Piersanti, their founder and spiritual guide, as our editor. Steve helped conceptualize, coach, and challenge us to give our best. Steve, once again, a million thanks!

The fabulous BK team under David Marshall, CEO, has been hugely invested in our success. We thank Jeevan Sivasubramaniam, editorial managing director, for his exceptional insights, Michael Crowley for peerless sales and marketing leadership, Katie Sheehan for brilliant media and publicity, Kristen Frantz for outstanding marketing strategies, Edward Wade for superb design and production, Leslie Crandell for making our lives so easy on US sales and support, Maria Jesus Aguilo, the best there on international sales, and Catherine Lengronne for amazing work on translation rights. Ashley Ingram's wonderful work on the cover is out there for all to see. It's wonderful to be in the hands of the best out there.

Our deepest appreciation to Roger Martin, renowned educator, business adviser, author of several bestselling books, and one of the world's most awarded management thinkers, for making an exception in agreeing to write the foreword.

Our colleagues at Inixia were incredibly supportive and helpful at every stage. We thank Dr. Vinisha Peres, Renaissance Woman, for research and editing. Richard Lancaster, Kip Fanta, David Cohen, Puneet

Aggarwal, Kathy Priest, Lisa Popyk, Christine Dauenhauer, Caroline Tooley, Ashley Martin, and Toby Lancaster—it's hard to overstate how much we appreciate your companionship and support.

Yazdi Bagli, Caroline Basyn, and Francisco Fraga—big thanks for your success stories and insights. BK's expert-network reviewers Simon J. Blattner III, Lesley Gale, and Sue Muehlbach provided extremely helpful comments that helped shape this book tremendously. To Rajan and Alka Panandiker, thank you for your huge investment of skill and time.

Several experts in the field took on the challenge of critiquing the manuscript in its early stage. Not only were they unfazed by the effort, but they also went above and beyond in shaping the insights in the book. Anupam Govil, Angela Pitasi, Ann Reilly, Anshul Srivastava, Beth Pohlmeyer, Brent Duersch, Carlos Amesquita, Carlos Yevara, Eric Levine, German Faraoni, Ganadeep Rey Patlolla, Hari Ram Eshwara, Josue Alencar, Marcello Zelioli, Mark Voytek, Mattijs Kersten, Michal Monit, Mike Lingle, Naomi Secor, Nicolas Kerling, Renu Singh, Sanjay Jiandani, Sarma Tekumalla, Simon Lant, Sudhir Kumar, Suman Sasmal, Sunil Malhotra, Varun Bhatia, and Vikrant Gadgil—we truly appreciate your contribution.

And finally, closest to our hearts, are our families. True to our respective cultures, they have provided an unlimited support platform for everything we do.

Tony would like to thank his parents, Ernest and Veronica Saldanha, for their endless support and love. His siblings and their spouses Marilyn and Ambrose, Ivy and Charles, Flory and Clifford for showing that physical distances are meaningless when it comes to being there. His daughters, Lara and Rene for the constant inspiration and learning. They continue to be models for how to follow your passion and how to make a difference. And, as always, a very special thanks to his wife Julia, for the ideas, collaboration, and attention to detail. This book wouldn't be the same without her help.

Filippo would like to thank his wife Lucia for her unconditional love and support over the past 44 years. His children Marta, Chiara, and

Emanuele for being a constant source of inspiration, both in thinking and in values. With them, their wonderful spouses and partner Jorge, Francesco, and Maris. Without all of them this book would not have happened.

Finally, he would like to thank his parents, Mario Passerini and Elvezia Equizi, as well as several spiritual guides he was fortunate to meet during his youth, for pointing him to the "North Star" of life.

INDEX

Page numbers followed by *f* reference figures.

ABOUT THE AUTHORS

We have always felt that despite having grown up in very different parts of the world—India and Italy—the two of us have much in common. On the professional front, we have both embraced dynamic, fast-changing experiences throughout our lives. We like to think of ourselves as being grounded change-leaders. Grounded in the sense that our skills lie in running large operations. However, our nature is to constantly question the status quo.

That transformative streak was evident in Tony's first book, *Why Digital Transformations Fail*. The focus of that book was on disciplined approaches to escape the 70% failure rate of digital transformations. It was a significant commercial success, with translations in six languages. That led to a further insight that although digital technology gets the exciting press, there is an equal opportunity for organizations around process transformation. That was not unexpected, since the majority of Tony's prior experience, including 35-plus years in the Global Business Services (GBS) industry, was related to transforming operations. During a 27-year career at Procter & Gamble he ran both operations and transformation for P&G's renowned GBS and IT organizations in every region of the world, ending up as Global Shared Services and Information Technology Senior Vice-President. As a well-known industry thought-leader he has led GBS design and operations, held CIO positions, managed acquisitions and divestitures, run large-scale outsourcing, created industry-wide disruptive innovation structures, and designed new business models. He was named on *Computerworld*'s Premier 100 IT Professionals list in 2013.

Tony has advised boards and c-suite executives around the world, including in more than twenty Fortune 500 companies. He's a globally sought-after keynote speaker in his spare time. Tony also advises several startups and venture capitalists. He has been on the advisory boards of several large tech companies. Among not-for-profits, Tony was the founding member and Chairman of the Board for the INTER-alliance of Greater Cincinnati, has chaired the board of Community Shares of Greater Cincinnati, and is a board member of Remineralize the Earth. Tony and his wife Julia have two daughters. They reside in Cincinnati, Ohio.

Filippo is a world-renowned executive. He coined the term Global Business Services (GBS), which is now commonly used to describe the more mature shared services organizations. He has won numerous awards (CIO of the Year, CIO Hall of Fame, Shared Service Thought Leader of the Year, Breakaway Leader Award, etc.) for having shaped the shared services and IT functions within their respective industries. His leadership work as President of Procter & Gamble's Global Business Services and Chief Information Officer has been recognized as best-in-class in the industry.

Filippo credits his upbringing and subsequent globe-trotting experience at P&G for shaping his intellectual curiosity and strategic thinking. He grew up in Rome, and his subsequent 33 years with P&G had him live in six countries across three continents, ultimately leading an organization across 70 countries. Filippo believes that his varied experiences are the key to his deep interest in business transformation, for which he is recognized worldwide. His nature is to constantly seek to understand the contextual elements around him that influence his decisions. Filippo is a master at turning empirical experience—that is, what we live and practice—into systems and models. The former without the latter is anecdotal; it may make interesting stories for people to listen to, but that experience is not easily reapplicable.

Filippo's strategies, principles, and ideas have been the subject of numerous books, articles, and *Harvard Business Reviews*. His organizations, as well as business models, have been recognized as best-in-class in their business domains. Filippo currently serves as a consultant to several companies and c-suite executives. He is an educator and board member of public and private companies. Filippo and his wife, Lucia, have three children. They live in New York City and Rome.

Revolutionizing Business Operations is thus the synthesis of a combined seven decades of practical executive experience, embracing of constant change, and the inclination to turn experiences into models. Our hope is that this book, along with our company Inixia, continues to provide the foundation for the next generation of executives to keep building on these models.

Berrett–Koehler
Publishers

Berrett-Koehler is an independent publisher dedicated to an ambitious mission: *Connecting people and ideas to create a world that works for all.*

Our publications span many formats, including print, digital, audio, and video. We also offer online resources, training, and gatherings. And we will continue expanding our products and services to advance our mission.

We believe that the solutions to the world's problems will come from all of us, working at all levels: in our society, in our organizations, and in our own lives. Our publications and resources offer pathways to creating a more just, equitable, and sustainable society. They help people make their organizations more humane, democratic, diverse, and effective (and we don't think there's any contradiction there). And they guide people in creating positive change in their own lives and aligning their personal practices with their aspirations for a better world.

And we strive to practice what we preach through what we call "The BK Way." At the core of this approach is *stewardship,* a deep sense of responsibility to administer the company for the benefit of all of our stakeholder groups, including authors, customers, employees, investors, service providers, sales partners, and the communities and environment around us. Everything we do is built around stewardship and our other core values of *quality, partnership, inclusion,* and *sustainability.*

This is why Berrett-Koehler is the first book publishing company to be both a B Corporation (a rigorous certification) and a benefit corporation (a for-profit legal status), which together require us to adhere to the highest standards for corporate, social, and environmental performance. And it is why we have instituted many pioneering practices (which you can learn about at www.bkconnection.com), including the Berrett-Koehler Constitution, the Bill of Rights and Responsibilities for BK Authors, and our unique Author Days.

We are grateful to our readers, authors, and other friends who are supporting our mission. We ask you to share with us examples of how BK publications and resources are making a difference in your lives, organizations, and communities at www.bkconnection.com/impact.

Dear reader,

Thank you for picking up this book and welcome to the worldwide BK community! You're joining a special group of people who have come together to create positive change in their lives, organizations, and communities.

What's BK all about?

Our mission is to connect people and ideas to create a world that works for all.

Why? Our communities, organizations, and lives get bogged down by old paradigms of self-interest, exclusion, hierarchy, and privilege. But we believe that can change. That's why we seek the leading experts on these challenges—and share their actionable ideas with you.

A welcome gift

To help you get started, we'd like to offer you a **free copy** of one of our bestselling ebooks:

www.bkconnection.com/welcome

When you claim your **free ebook**, you'll also be subscribed to our blog.

Our freshest insights

Access the best new tools and ideas for leaders at all levels on our blog at ideas.bkconnection.com.

Sincerely,

Your friends at Berrett-Koehler

Certified

Corporation